The end was my beginning

Dedication

To my Heavenly Father, whose unwavering grace and boundless mercy pulled me from the depths of despair and guided me onto the path of redemption. Without Your divine intervention, this story would have ended far differently. This book is a testament to Your power, Your love, and Your infinite capacity for forgiveness. To my family and friends, who, despite my failings, continued to offer their support, their prayers, and their unwavering belief in my ability to heal. Your patience, your understanding, and your steadfast love were the lifeline that kept me afloat during the darkest storms. Your forgiveness, freely given, was the balm that soothed my wounded soul. This book is dedicated to each of you, a small token of my immeasurable gratitude. And to all those struggling with addiction, with despair, with the crushing weight of their past: know that you are not alone. There is hope. There is healing. There is redemption. Believe in the power of faith, the strength of perseverance, and the transformative potential of God's love.

Preface

Writing this memoir has been a journey in itself—a process of confronting long-buried demons, of excavating the painful memories that shaped my past, and of wrestling with the raw emotions that still linger within. It wasn't easy to revisit the darkness that once consumed me, to relive the moments of despair and desperation, the agonizing struggles against addiction's relentless grip. But in sharing my story, I hope to offer a glimmer of light, a beacon of hope for others who feel trapped in the shadows of their own battles. This is not a story of self-pity or blame. It's not a tale designed to evoke shock or sensationalize the horrors of addiction. Rather, it's a testament to the incredible power of faith, the transformative potential of grace, and the enduring strength of the human spirit. It is a story of a woman who, through the mercy of God and the unwavering support of those who loved her, found a path out of the abyss, a path that led her to healing, redemption, and ultimately, a life of purpose. My hope is that this book will inspire others to find the courage to face their own struggles, to seek help, and to believe that even in the deepest darkness, there is always a light waiting to be discovered.

Introduction

The road to redemption is rarely a straight line. Mine was a treacherous, winding path, littered with obstacles and pitfalls, punctuated by moments of profound despair and unexpected grace. This memoir chronicles that journey—from the initial whispers of addiction that lured me into its insidious grasp, to the devastating consequences that followed, to the miraculous turning point that transformed my life. It is a story of loss and recovery, of brokenness and healing, of darkness and light. I share my experiences with complete honesty, not to solicit sympathy, but to offer a realistic portrayal of the struggle against addiction. It's a battle fought not only against a substance, but against a deep-seated sense of self-loathing, against the insidious lies that addiction whispers into the heart, and against the powerful forces of despair. But this is also a story of faith, a testament to the power of unwavering belief in a higher power and the transformative effect of surrendering one's life to God's grace. It is a testament to the importance of community, to the healing power of forgiveness, and to the unwavering support of those who believe in our potential even when we ourselves have lost hope. It is the story of a life reborn, a testament to the unwavering truth that even amidst seemingly insurmountable odds, transformation and hope are possible. What follows is not simply a recounting of events, but an exploration of the emotions, the thoughts, and the spiritual battles that defined my struggle and ultimately led me to a life beyond my wildest dreams. It is my prayer that this story will resonate with readers, offering solace, inspiration, and the unwavering assurance that true and lasting transformation is always possible.

The Early Years and the Seeds of Despair

My earliest memories are etched in the sepia tones of a small, cramped house in a town that felt perpetually shrouded in mist. The air hung heavy with the scent of damp earth and woodsmoke, a smell that, even now, can transport me back to those years with unsettling clarity. It wasn't a cruel childhood, not overtly, but it was one marked by a pervasive sense of unease, a feeling of being perpetually off-kilter. My parents, though loving in their own way, were products of their time, a generation that didn't readily express emotion. Affection was shown through acts of service, not words of affirmation, a language I struggled to decipher as a child. My father, a hardworking man consumed by the relentless demands of his job, was often distant, his silences more profound than any harsh words. My mother, burdened by the weight of unspoken expectations, carried a quiet sadness that I sensed intuitively, a melancholic undercurrent that permeated our home.

The house itself felt oppressive, a reflection perhaps of the emotional climate within. The walls were thin, every creak and groan amplifying the silence, every whispered argument echoing in the cramped spaces. We lived on a quiet street, but the stillness was deceptive. It concealed a simmering tension, a sense of unspoken anxieties that hung in the air like a suffocating blanket. I remember the constant fear of disappointing my parents, a fear that stemmed not from overt discipline but from a subtle, unspoken pressure to conform to their unspoken expectations. Their expectations, while not explicitly stated, were heavy with the weight of a past I didn't fully understand. Their silence spoke volumes, painting a picture of a life lived with quiet desperation, a struggle to find joy in the mundane routine.

The lack of open communication created a chasm between me and my parents. I yearned for connection, for understanding, but my attempts to bridge the gap often met with stony silence or vague dismissals. As a result, I retreated into myself, building an invisible wall around my emotions. This emotional isolation became a fertile ground for anxieties to take root and flourish. The smallest criticisms, the slightest disappointments, were magnified in the echo chamber of my own mind, leaving me feeling inadequate, unworthy of love and acceptance. I longed for a sense of belonging, a feeling of being seen and understood, a yearning that would later manifest in unhealthy ways. The foundation of my self-esteem was shaky at best, built on shifting sands of parental approval I never felt fully secured.

This internal struggle manifested itself in various ways. I was a shy, introverted child, often lost in the world of books, finding solace in imaginary realms where I could create a sense of belonging I lacked in reality. School was a mixed experience. While I excelled academically, navigating the social complexities of the schoolyard proved challenging. I was neither popular nor unpopular, more like a silent observer, watching the ebb and flow of friendships with a mixture of envy and detachment. The fear of rejection was a constant companion, a shadow that clung to me, whispering doubts and insecurities. I lacked the confidence to reach out, to make genuine connections, to expose my vulnerabilities.

One particular incident stands out with stark clarity. I was in the fifth grade when a group of older girls, fueled by adolescent cruelty, targeted me with relentless teasing. Their taunts, petty and seemingly insignificant, left deep scars. The words they hurled at me resonated within me long after they were spoken, reinforcing the feelings of inadequacy that had already taken root. I remember feeling utterly alone, utterly helpless against the wave of their cruelty, my silence amplifying their power. This experience left me with a profound sense of vulnerability, a feeling of being exposed and defenseless. It's a feeling that would haunt me for years to come, a deep-seated fear of judgment and rejection that would contribute significantly to my later self-destructive behavior.

The emotional turmoil of my childhood wasn't confined to the schoolyard. At home, the tensions between my parents often reached a boiling point, though rarely expressed openly. Arguments were muffled, hushed affairs, punctuated by slammed doors and strained silences. The underlying conflict, whatever its nature, left a lingering sense of instability and uncertainty. I felt the weight of their unspoken anxieties pressing down on me, a heavy blanket of unresolved emotions. It was as if the walls of our home were not only physically cramped, but also emotionally suffocating. I yearned for a sense of peace, a feeling of security, but instead, I lived in a state of constant low-level anxiety, always anticipating the next eruption of conflict, the next unspoken disapproval.

The lack of emotional support from my family left me searching for external validation, a desperate need to feel seen, heard, and accepted. This need, unfortunately, would lead me down a path of self-destruction. The seeds of my despair, sown in the fertile ground of my childhood experiences, would eventually blossom into a full-blown addiction, a desperate attempt to escape the pain and loneliness that had become my constant companions. My early years were not simply a prelude to my addiction; they were its foundation, the cracked and uneven ground upon which the edifice of my self-destruction would be built. The unspoken anxieties, the silences, the lack of emotional connection, all contributed to the vulnerability that would eventually lead me to seek solace in the fleeting oblivion offered by drugs. This is not an attempt to excuse my actions, but rather to offer a glimpse into the complex interplay of factors that led to my descent into darkness. It's a story that must be told, not as a justification, but as a testament to the profound power of faith and redemption.

The feeling of being adrift, of lacking a stable anchor in my life, was a constant undercurrent in those early years. There was a profound loneliness, a sense of disconnection not only from my parents but also from myself. I felt like an outsider looking in, observing my own life with a detached curiosity, unable to fully participate in my own experience. This alienation, this profound sense of being alone in a crowded world, would eventually lead me to seek comfort in the false embrace of addiction. The fleeting escape it offered, the illusion of connection, proved alluring, a siren song that lured me into a treacherous sea of self-destruction. It's crucial to understand this context, this tapestry of unmet needs and unspoken anxieties, to comprehend the depth of my despair and the intensity of my craving for something, anything, to fill the void within.

This wasn't a sudden fall, but a gradual descent, a slow erosion of my self-worth and sense of purpose. The subtle shifts, the slow accumulation of negative experiences, these were the building blocks of my addiction, each contributing to the crumbling foundation of my life. My early years weren't defined by dramatic trauma, but by a constant, low-level hum of discontent, a pervasive sense of unease that would eventually overwhelm me. Understanding this is vital to understanding my story, to appreciating the depth of the darkness I fell into, and the magnitude of the journey back towards the light. The journey wasn't simply about overcoming addiction; it was about confronting the core wounds of my childhood, healing the emotional scars that had made me so vulnerable in the first place. It was about reclaiming my life, my identity, my very soul. And in the telling of this story, I hope to offer not only my personal testimony, but a message of hope to others who may be struggling in the darkness, lost in the shadows of their own pasts.

The Allure of Addiction and the First Taste of Escape

The first time I touched it, it wasn't a conscious decision. It wasn't a rebellious act, a desperate cry for attention, or even a calculated attempt at self-destruction. It was… curiosity. A whisper in the shadows of my already fragile self-esteem, a fleeting notion that maybe, just maybe, this could be an answer. A way to silence the relentless hum of anxiety that had become the soundtrack of my life. It was offered casually, almost carelessly, by someone I considered a friend. A friend who, in retrospect, I can see was as lost as I was, adrift in the same sea of unspoken anxieties and unmet needs.

The initial effect was disorienting, a strange mix of exhilaration and confusion. The world seemed to soften around the edges, the harsh lines of reality blurring into a hazy, dreamlike state. The anxieties that usually gnawed at my insides, the relentless self-doubt, the constant feeling of inadequacy – they seemed to recede, to fade into the background noise of my consciousness. It was a temporary reprieve, a brief escape from the relentless pressure I felt to be someone I wasn't. It was a momentary feeling of lightness, of freedom from the suffocating weight of my own self-consciousness.

That first experience wasn't about escape, not entirely. It was more about a subtle shift in perspective, a temporary alteration of my internal landscape. The world suddenly felt more manageable, less threatening. The anxieties still existed, but they were muted, dulled, as if viewed through a frosted glass. It was a deceptive calm, a false sense of peace, but in that moment, it was enough. It was a taste of something different, something that promised solace from the relentless storm raging within me.

The second time was easier. The hesitation, the initial uncertainty, was gone, replaced by a familiar yearning, a subtle craving for that altered state of being. The escape, though temporary, had been enticing enough to make me want to experience it again. This time, the effect was more pronounced. The blurring of reality was more intense, the sense of detachment more profound. I felt unburdened, released from the weight of my self-consciousness, free from the judgmental gaze that I had always felt keenly.

This pattern continued, a slow, insidious escalation. Each subsequent experience brought with it a deepening sense of dependence, a growing need for that temporary oblivion. The intervals between use shortened, the doses increased. What began as a fleeting curiosity transformed into a desperate need, a compulsive craving that overshadowed everything else in my life. The allure of the drug grew stronger, its promise of escape more seductive, more irresistible. It became my refuge, my sanctuary, my escape from the pain, the loneliness, the crippling self-doubt that had become my constant companions.

The changes were subtle at first, almost imperceptible. But as the addiction took hold, they became more pronounced, more undeniable. My priorities shifted. Things that once held importance – school, my relationships, my aspirations – began to fade into the background, eclipsed by the overwhelming need to obtain and use the drug. The sense of urgency intensified, consuming my thoughts, dictating my actions. Everything else became secondary, a mere distraction from the relentless pursuit of my next high.

The sensory experiences associated with the drug became deeply ingrained, etched into the very fabric of my being. I remember the metallic taste, the burning sensation as it went down, the almost immediate rush of euphoria. I remember the distorted perceptions, the heightened senses, the altered sense of time. The world would morph and twist, colors becoming more vivid, sounds more intense, smells more potent. It was a world of heightened sensations, a hallucinatory realm where reality was malleable, where I could escape the confines of my own mind.

But the euphoria was fleeting, always followed by the crash, the inevitable descent into a state of exhaustion, anxiety, and depression. The lows became increasingly profound, the periods of sobriety more agonizing. The cycle continued, a relentless pattern of highs and lows, of intoxication and withdrawal, a self-inflicted torture that I seemed powerless to stop.

The emotional and psychological changes were even more devastating. My self-esteem plummeted. I felt worthless, ashamed, and utterly alone. The relationships I had once valued began to crumble, replaced by a sense of isolation and paranoia. The world became a hostile place, a landscape filled with judgment and condemnation. I retreated further into myself, hiding my addiction from those I loved, deepening the isolation that had already become a defining feature of my life.

My sense of self eroded, my identity fragmented. The person I was before, the person I had hoped to become – these faded into distant memories, replaced by a sense of emptiness, a void that nothing seemed to fill. The drug offered a temporary respite from this emptiness, a fleeting illusion of wholeness, but it only served to exacerbate the underlying issues, deepening the chasm between me and myself.

The conflict within me raged. I knew what I was doing was wrong, destructive. I knew I needed to stop, that I was hurting myself and those around me. But the grip of addiction was too strong, the craving too intense, the fear of withdrawal too paralyzing. I felt trapped, caught in a vicious cycle, unable to break free from the chains of my own self-destruction. The guilt, the shame, the self-loathing – these were constant companions, gnawing at my soul, fueling the despair that drove me further into the depths of addiction. I was drowning, and the more I struggled, the deeper I sank. Each attempt to climb back to the surface only resulted in a more devastating fall. I felt like a prisoner of my own mind, my own body, my own devastating choices. The darkness was complete, encompassing, suffocating. I was lost, completely and utterly lost.

The Crumbling Foundation Relationships and Consequences

The first cracks appeared in my relationship with my mother. It wasn't a sudden shattering, but a slow, insidious erosion, like the relentless drip of water wearing away at stone. Initially, she'd expressed concern, her worry etched into the lines around her eyes, the tremor in her voice. She'd ask about my late nights, the changes in my appearance – the gauntness, the perpetual shadows under my eyes, the clothes that hung loosely on my shrinking frame. I'd deflect her questions, offering vague excuses, my lies tumbling out effortlessly, practiced and polished from years of hiding my true self.

The lies, however, became more frequent, more elaborate, more desperate. They were a necessary shield, a fragile defense against the truth, a truth that would shatter the already precarious foundation of our relationship. The deception created a chasm between us, a space filled with unspoken accusations, simmering resentments, and the cold, hard silence that spoke volumes more than any shouted argument could have.

Her attempts to reach me became increasingly frantic, punctuated by tearful pleas and whispered prayers. The worry in her eyes deepened, transforming into a profound sadness that mirrored the growing despair within me. I saw the pain I caused reflected in her face, yet I was powerless to stop, too consumed by my own self-destruction to acknowledge the damage I was inflicting on the woman who had loved me unconditionally. The guilt gnawed at me, a relentless worm boring its way into my soul, but it was a guilt I carefully buried beneath layers of denial and self-justification.

The deterioration of my relationship with my sister was more abrupt, a sudden, violent rupture. She'd witnessed my descent firsthand, seeing the transformation from a vibrant, hopeful young woman into a hollow shell, haunted by shadows and consumed by cravings. She'd tried to intervene, her words a mixture of concern and anger, her attempts to help met with defensiveness and hostility. Her attempts at intervention felt like accusations, and her compassion felt like judgment.

One particularly volatile confrontation stands out in my memory. I remember her eyes, filled with a mixture of pain and disgust, as she confronted me about my behavior, about the lies, the disappearances, the erratic moods. The anger in her voice was raw, unfiltered, a fierce protectiveness that was both heartbreaking and terrifying. My response was a furious denial, a desperate attempt to push her away before she could witness the full extent of my self-destruction. That was the last time we spoke for an extended period.

My friendships fared no better. My once-vibrant social life crumbled, replaced by a sense of isolation and paranoia. The friends who had once been a constant presence in my life gradually drifted away, their attempts to maintain contact met with indifference or outright hostility. Their concerns seemed like intrusions, their attempts at friendship, a betrayal of the secret world I had created for myself. I alienated them, pushing them away before they could witness my disintegration, my descent into the abyss.

The familiar haunts of my addiction became my new social circles. The dingy bars, the dimly lit alleys, the shadowy corners – these were the places where I sought refuge, where

I felt a perverse sense of belonging among other lost souls, drowning in their own despair. These locations became the stage for my most desperate acts, for the most shameful moments.

The physical environment played a significant role in my descent. The dingy motel rooms where I'd spend nights, the squalid apartments, the abandoned buildings – these places mirrored my inner state, a reflection of the decay and desolation that had consumed my life. The stale air hung heavy with the stench of stale beer, cigarette smoke, and desperation, permeating every fiber of my being. These places were silent witnesses to my self-destruction, silent accomplices in my downward spiral.

The consequences were far-reaching, affecting every aspect of my life. My academic career ended abruptly, my dreams of a future dashed against the rocks of my addiction. My financial situation deteriorated, my resources depleted as I prioritised my habit over all else. The shame and guilt became unbearable, crushing weights that threatened to suffocate me completely. I felt trapped, a prisoner in my own mind, a victim of my own choices.

The isolation was profound, a complete severance from the life I had once known. The world seemed to shrink, constricting around me, leaving me feeling alone, adrift in a sea of despair. Even the few people who remained in my life became distant figures, viewed through a lens of mistrust and paranoia. The constant fear of exposure amplified my already intense feelings of guilt and shame, creating a vicious cycle of self-destruction.

There were moments of clarity, fleeting glimpses of the person I once was, a woman filled with hope, ambition, and dreams. These moments were brief, however, quickly overshadowed by the overwhelming desire to escape the pain, the emptiness, the relentless self-loathing that consumed me. These moments served only to amplify the feeling of my failure, the realization of how far I had fallen, how much I had lost.

The damage I inflicted on those who loved me was immeasurable. The pain in my mother's eyes, the silent anger in my sister's, the disappointment in the faces of my friends – these are images that continue to haunt me, a constant reminder of the destructive power of addiction. The trust was broken, the bonds severed, the relationships shattered beyond repair. The guilt and remorse, for the pain and damage inflicted, continue to be a significant part of my healing journey. The path to redemption was long and arduous, paved with moments of despair and punctuated by the unwavering presence of faith. The road to healing has been arduous and ongoing, but my faith remains the guiding light, illuminating the path towards redemption. This is a journey of continuous transformation.

Hitting Rock Bottom Despair and the Threat of Death

The relentless cycle of addiction had finally caught up with me. My body, once a vessel of vibrant energy, was now a decaying ruin, ravaged by neglect and abuse. The constant cravings, the sleepless nights, the relentless pursuit of the next fix had taken their toll. My skin, once clear and smooth, was now sallow and blotchy, marred by track marks that served as a grotesque map of my self-destruction. My teeth ached, my gums bled, my breath reeked of decay. I was a walking corpse, a testament to the destructive power of addiction.

One particular evening, the blur of days and nights coalescing into a single, unending torment, found me collapsed in a dingy alleyway, the cold concrete a stark contrast to the burning fever that consumed me. The world swam before my eyes, a kaleidoscope of distorted colors and sounds. My breath came in ragged gasps, each inhalation a struggle, each exhalation a release of the poison that coursed through my veins. I lay there, helpless, utterly alone, my body wracked with pain, my mind consumed by a profound and soul-crushing despair.

This wasn't just physical discomfort; it was a profound, existential weariness, a bone-deep exhaustion that transcended the physical realm. It was the despair of a soul stripped bare, a spirit broken beyond repair. I had no hope left, no desire to fight, no will to live. I was merely existing, drifting through a landscape of unrelenting darkness, a shadow of the person I once was. My spirit was fractured, my will broken, my heart a desolate wasteland.

The memory of my mother's face, etched with worry and grief, flickered through my clouded mind. The image of my sister's anger, her disappointment, the coldness that had settled between us; it all washed over me in waves of agonizing guilt and self-loathing. The faces of my friends, once bright and familiar, were now distant and blurred, replaced by the faces of the other lost souls I found myself surrounded by in my addiction.

I remember a fleeting thought – a stark, horrifying realization that I was dying. Not a sudden, dramatic end, but a slow, agonizing fade into nothingness. A realization that struck with chilling clarity amidst the fog of my addiction. The thought wasn't terrifying in a visceral sense, more like a weary acceptance. It was as if a part of me had already surrendered, conceding to the inevitable end.

That night, or perhaps it was a series of nights blurred together in the haze of my addiction, marked a turning point. I ended up in the emergency room, not from an intentional overdose, but from a cascade of complications arising from years of neglect and abuse. My body was simply shutting down, overwhelmed by the constant assault of toxins and the lack of basic care.

The fluorescent lights of the hospital room, the antiseptic smell, the rhythmic beep of the heart monitor – these were jarring intrusions into the darkness that had become my reality. The sterile environment felt alien, a stark contrast to the grime and squalor I had become accustomed to. The faces of doctors and nurses, their expressions a mixture of concern and pity, were both unnerving and strangely comforting.

For the first time in a long time, I felt a glimmer of something akin to hope – not a vibrant, life-affirming hope, but a fragile spark in the suffocating darkness. It was the hope of survival, a base instinct to cling to life, an involuntary reflex in the face of oblivion.

Days bled into weeks. My stay at the hospital was long, punctuated by moments of lucidity, clarity that pierced through the haze of addiction. During those moments of lucidity, I could see the depths of my degradation. I remember the stark terror that washed over me at the realization that this was where my life had led me – to a hospital bed, a broken body, and the cold reality of my impending death if I didn't change.

It was in those sterile white walls, surrounded by the sounds of life support machines and the hushed tones of medical professionals, that the seeds of change were sown. The fear of death was a powerful catalyst, a stark reminder of the preciousness of life, a life I had so recklessly thrown away. It was a brutal awakening, a jarring confrontation with my own mortality.

The physical pain was intense, a constant reminder of the damage I had inflicted upon myself. The withdrawal symptoms were excruciating. Each shiver, each ache, each spasm was a testament to the insidious power of addiction, a brutal reminder of the consequences of my choices. I was stripped bare, exposed, vulnerable, and utterly dependent on the care of others.

During my hospital stay, I had little to distract me from the overwhelming sense of my own failure. The weight of my actions bore down on me, the broken relationships, the lost opportunities, the pain I had caused those I loved. The guilt was a physical entity, crushing me, suffocating me, a reminder of the havoc I'd wreaked. The shame was a brand, seared into my soul.

The feeling of isolation, previously self-imposed, became a tangible thing in the hospital, different from the self-imposed isolation of addiction. It was the quiet desperation of knowing that I had lost everything - my health, my relationships, my future – and that I was responsible for it. The silence was deafening. The silence was a symphony of the self-loathing and regret.

Yet, amidst the pain and despair, a tiny flicker of faith began to rekindle. It was a faint ember, threatened constantly by the winds of doubt and self-recrimination, yet stubbornly refusing to be extinguished. It wasn't a sudden, dramatic conversion, but a gradual, incremental shift in my perspective, a slow awakening to the possibility of redemption.

The nurses, the doctors, the therapists I interacted with during my hospital stay, even in their professional roles, showed a compassion and empathy I had rarely encountered during my addiction. This unexpected kindness began to chip away at the hardened shell of cynicism and despair that had encased my heart. They demonstrated faith in me when I lacked faith in myself, an act of faith I started to see as mirroring the faith of the God I had forgotten. This faith, in all its surprising places, was the first small step towards a long and difficult journey of healing and redemption. My journey toward God was born from an unlikely place, a sterile hospital room, filled with the sounds of life-support machines, but the seeds were sown. I was far from home, but I was beginning to find my way back. The road ahead remained daunting, but for the first time in a long time, I saw a path, however dimly lit, leading away from the abyss.

A Glimmer of Hope The First Seeds of Change

The antiseptic smell of the hospital room, initially jarring, began to feel less alien, less threatening. The rhythmic beep of the heart monitor, once a symbol of my failing body, became a strangely comforting metronome marking the passage of time, a time I was now, for the first time in years, allowing myself to inhabit. Days turned into weeks, the initial acute phase of withdrawal slowly giving way to a protracted struggle against the insidious cravings. The physical discomfort remained, a constant, nagging reminder of the damage I had inflicted upon myself, but the sharp edges of the pain were beginning to dull. The excruciating withdrawal symptoms, the relentless waves of nausea, the bone-deep aches, the debilitating tremors – these slowly began to subside, replaced by a persistent, weary exhaustion.

During those long, quiet hours, with little to distract me from the echoing silence of the room, my mind began to wander. Memories, long suppressed, surfaced unexpectedly, shattering the carefully constructed walls of denial I had erected around my past. I recalled my childhood, the warmth of my mother's embrace, the laughter shared with my sister, the feeling of belonging within a loving family. These memories, once sources of comfort, now felt like ghosts, taunting me with the stark contrast between my past and my present. The guilt, the shame, the overwhelming sense of loss – these were not abstract concepts but physical entities, heavy and suffocating, pressing down on me, constricting my breath.

One particular afternoon, a young volunteer, a girl barely older than my younger sister, came to visit. She brought with her a worn, paperback copy of the Psalms. I had always been vaguely familiar with the Bible, having grown up in a nominally Christian household, but religious faith had been absent from my life for years, a casualty of my addiction. I'd seen faith as weakness, a crutch for the unprepared. I took the book, not out of genuine interest, but out of a simple desire for a distraction from the torment of my own thoughts.

As I flipped through the pages, the words, though familiar, struck me with an unexpected power. The raw honesty of the Psalms, the lamentations, the pleas for forgiveness, the expressions of profound grief and despair – these resonated deeply within me. Here were words that mirrored my own internal turmoil, articulating the pain, the anguish, the sense of utter hopelessness that I had been struggling to express. It was a language of desperation that I could understand, a voice that spoke directly to my soul.

It wasn't a sudden epiphany, a dramatic conversion experience. It was far subtler than that. It was simply a recognition that I wasn't alone in my suffering. That others, before me, had experienced similar depths of despair and had found solace, hope, and a path toward healing. The Psalms didn't offer easy answers, didn't magically erase the pain, but they offered a connection, a sense of shared humanity, a validation of my suffering. It was a recognition that my pain, my anguish, was not meaningless, not inconsequential, not something to be ignored or suppressed. It was something to be acknowledged, embraced, and poured out.

That evening, after the volunteer had left, I began to read aloud, my voice raspy and weak, the words stumbling out between gasps of air. I read of David's repentance, his cries for mercy, his profound expressions of grief and despair. And as I read, something shifted within me. A quiet, inner peace, a gentle sense of acceptance, began to seep into the desolate wasteland of my heart.

The nurses and doctors, observing my change, couldn't quite place it. They saw a physical improvement, of course, but they also noticed a subtle shift in my demeanor. The pervasive despair that had clung to me like a shroud seemed to be lifting, replaced by a tentative glimmer of hope. They were witnessing a transformation, a resurrection of sorts, but they couldn't explain it. I couldn't either. It was a mystery unfolding, a healing that started not with understanding, but with trust.

One of the nurses, a kindly woman with a gentle smile and eyes that seemed to see right through me, sensed my growing connection with the Psalms. She suggested I attend a church service when I was well enough to leave the hospital. The idea initially filled me with dread. The thought of entering a church, a place I had associated with hypocrisy and judgment, was uncomfortable. Yet, the very discomfort, the very fear, held a strange appeal. It was a challenge, a test of my newfound courage.

The time I spent in the hospital was a crucible, forging me anew in the fires of suffering and testing the limits of my endurance. The physical pain was only part of the battle; the emotional and spiritual struggles were far more intense, far more draining. The withdrawal symptoms, though excruciating, were nothing compared to the relentless onslaught of guilt, shame, and self-loathing that gnawed at my soul. Yet, amidst the darkness, a tiny spark of hope began to glow, fueled by the unexpected kindness of others, the comfort found in the Psalms, and the nascent stirring of faith.

The weeks that followed my release from the hospital were a blur of doctor's appointments, therapy sessions, and a slow, painstaking process of rebuilding my life, brick by brick. The physical recovery was gradual, agonizingly slow, but the emotional and spiritual healing seemed to be happening at an accelerated pace. My newfound faith, fragile as it was, became a lifeline, anchoring me during the tumultuous storms that continued to rage within me.

The early days were challenging, punctuated by moments of doubt, moments when the darkness threatened to engulf me once more. The cravings returned, though less intense, less frequent. The memories of my past, once sources of shame and guilt, were beginning to transform into opportunities for forgiveness and redemption. The relationships I had damaged began to slowly heal, nurtured by acts of contrition and a commitment to making amends.

My path to recovery wasn't a linear journey. There were setbacks, relapses, and moments of profound despair. Yet, amidst the turmoil, faith remained, a constant beacon illuminating the way forward. It was a faith that was born not from theological discussions or intellectual reasoning but from the raw, visceral experience of suffering and the unexpected discovery of compassion and hope in the most unlikely of places: a sterile hospital room, a worn paperback copy of the Psalms, and the kind eyes of a volunteer, a nurse, and a growing community of believers. The path ahead was long, and the climb steep, but the first steps had been taken. The first seeds of change had been planted, watered by tears, nurtured by faith, and blossoming slowly but surely in the fertile ground of my broken heart. The journey had begun.

The Unexpected Encounter A Chance for Redemption

It was a crisp autumn afternoon, the kind that paints the sky in hues of burnt orange and deep crimson. Released from the hospital a week prior, I was still weak, my body a fragile vessel barely holding its contents together. My therapist had suggested a walk in the park, a gentle nudge towards reintegrating into the world beyond the sterile confines of the medical facility. I shuffled along the paved path, my breath catching in my chest with each labored step. The vibrant colors of the falling leaves, usually a source of joy, felt muted, dulled by the persistent grayness that still clouded my mind. The world felt fragile, as fragile as I felt.

I had found a small measure of peace in the Psalms, a quiet solace in the words of ancient lamentations and heartfelt pleas for forgiveness. But the peace was precarious, a fragile butterfly fluttering on the edge of a storm. The cravings still lingered, phantom pains that danced along the edges of my consciousness. Sleep offered little respite, filled with nightmares that replayed my past mistakes in vivid, agonizing detail. The days bled into each other, a monotonous cycle of physical therapy, medication, and the crushing weight of my own guilt.

As I rounded a bend in the path, I saw him. He was an older gentleman, sitting on a park bench, his silver hair catching the afternoon sun. He was reading a book, his head slightly bowed, his expression serene. There was something about his posture, his stillness, that drew me in. Something in his quiet presence suggested a peace that I desperately craved. He was alone, yet he didn't seem lonely. He emanated a sense of contentment, a quiet joy that was strangely captivating.

Hesitantly, I approached him. The simple act of walking those few steps felt monumental, a Herculean effort that demanded every ounce of my remaining strength. My legs trembled, and I felt a familiar wave of nausea wash over me. But I pushed forward, driven by an inexplicable urge to connect, to share my burden with someone, anyone.

He looked up as I approached, his eyes, surprisingly bright and clear for a man of his age, meeting mine with a gentle understanding. There was no judgment in his gaze, no hint of condemnation. Only kindness, an acceptance that washed over me like a balm.

"Beautiful day, isn't it?" he said, his voice soft, his tone warm.

I managed a weak smile. "It is," I whispered, my voice trembling.

He nodded, gesturing to the bench beside him. "Care to sit?"

I sank onto the cold wood, the sudden stillness offering a momentary reprieve from the turmoil within. We sat in silence for a while, the rustling of leaves and the distant chirping of birds forming a gentle soundtrack to our shared solitude. I was acutely aware of my own ragged breathing, the tremor in my hands, the uneasy flutter in my chest. He noticed, I'm sure, but he said nothing.

Finally, I found myself confessing, spilling my story to this complete stranger – my addiction, my struggles, my despair, my newfound tentative faith. The words tumbled out, a torrent of confession, shame, and self-loathing. I had expected judgment, ridicule, maybe even pity. But instead, he listened, his gaze unwavering, his expression patient and understanding.

He didn't interrupt, didn't offer platitudes or facile advice. He simply listened, offering the profound gift of his undivided attention. And as I spoke, a strange thing happened. The weight of my guilt, the crushing burden of my past, seemed to lighten. The shame, that relentless tormentor that had pursued me for so long, began to lose its power. It was as if, by simply sharing my story, by allowing myself to be seen in my vulnerability, I was slowly, gradually, releasing the shackles of my self-imposed imprisonment.

When I had finished speaking, my voice hoarse and my eyes overflowing with tears, he placed a comforting hand on my arm. "You are not alone," he said softly. "God sees you. He loves you. And He wants to heal you."

His words, simple and unadorned, resonated deep within me. They were not theological pronouncements or intellectual arguments. They were words of profound compassion, a message of hope delivered with quiet conviction. I had been seeking answers, desperately searching for a solution to my problems, a cure for my spiritual malady. But what I found instead was something far more profound: unconditional love.

He didn't offer a quick fix or a theological debate. He simply shared his own journey of faith, his own struggles with temptation, his own moments of doubt. He spoke of grace, of redemption, of the transformative power of God's love. He shared stories of his own life, tales of hardship and perseverance, of setbacks and triumphs, each story weaving a tapestry of hope and resilience.

His words were a gentle reassurance, a quiet testament to the enduring power of faith. He spoke of the importance of forgiveness, both for myself and for those who had hurt me. He helped me understand that my past mistakes did not define me, that I was capable of change, of growth, of redemption.

As the sun began to dip below the horizon, casting long shadows across the park, I felt a sense of profound peace descend upon me. The darkness that had clung to me for so long began to recede, replaced by a tentative glimmer of hope. It wasn't a sudden, dramatic transformation, but a subtle shift, a quiet awakening.

He gave me his phone number, telling me to call if I ever needed anything, anytime. He didn't push his faith on me, yet his faith shone through his every action and word, and it was profoundly infectious. We walked to the edge of the park together, our parting a silent acknowledgement of the profound connection we had forged.

That evening, I sat by my window, watching the stars emerge in the darkening sky, a sense of profound gratitude swelling within my heart. I knew I had just encountered something special, something transformative. The encounter in the park wasn't just a random event; it was a pivotal moment, a divinely orchestrated rendezvous. It wasn't just a conversation; it was a turning point. I knew I had found a beacon, a light on the long, winding road ahead. The path to recovery was still long and arduous, but I was no longer walking it alone. I had found a guide, a friend, a fellow traveler. And more importantly, I had found the comfort and hope that faith offered, the transformative power of God's love. The unexpected encounter in the park was more than just a chance meeting; it was a chance for redemption, a pathway towards healing, a testament to the unwavering power of faith and the enduring kindness of strangers. The seeds of hope planted in the sterile environment of the hospital room were now flourishing, nurtured by faith, strengthened by compassion, and blossoming slowly but surely in the fertile ground of my newly awakened heart. The journey continued, but with each passing day, the path became clearer, the burden lighter, and the hope brighter.

Embracing Spirituality A New Foundation for Life

The park encounter had been a catalyst, igniting a spark of faith that I hadn't known I possessed. It wasn't a sudden, dramatic conversion, more like a slow dawning, a gradual unfolding of a truth I'd subconsciously suppressed for years. The man's kindness, his unwavering belief in my capacity for redemption, had chipped away at the hardened shell of cynicism and self-loathing that had encased my heart. I started small, attending a quiet church service a few weeks later. The stained-glass windows, bathed in the afternoon sun, seemed to cast a holy glow upon the congregation. The hymns, sung with heartfelt sincerity, resonated with my own quiet longing for peace. I felt an unfamiliar sense of belonging, a connection to something larger than myself, something profoundly healing.

Initially, the experience felt strangely disorienting. The whispers of doubt, the insidious voice of addiction, still lingered, casting shadows on my newfound hope. The familiar urge to retreat into the familiar darkness, to escape the vulnerability of faith, remained a persistent temptation. But the seeds of hope that the man in the park had planted were beginning to take root. I found myself drawn to scripture, finding solace in the Psalms, in the prophetic writings of Isaiah, and in the parables of Jesus. The words, once distant and irrelevant, now resonated with a profound personal meaning.

The words weren't just abstract theological concepts; they were stories of redemption, of forgiveness, of hope amidst despair. They spoke of a God who understood my struggles, a God who had seen the depths of my despair and yet still offered unconditional love and unwavering grace. The stories of others' struggles, their falls and their rises, their moments of doubt and their moments of profound faith, offered me a sense of community, a sense of belonging that I'd craved for so long. I wasn't alone in my struggle; millions had walked this path before me, and millions would walk it after. This realization was immensely comforting, a powerful antidote to the isolating shame and guilt that had consumed me for so long.

I started attending a weekly support group at the church. The shared vulnerability of the other attendees, their willingness to share their struggles and triumphs, created a powerful sense of solidarity. The group wasn't just about recovery from addiction; it was about forging a community of faith, a network of support and encouragement that helped to bolster my resolve. Listening to their stories, their testimonies of faith and healing, offered me both inspiration and validation. I was no longer fighting this battle alone; I had found allies, kindred spirits who understood the depths of my struggle and the complexities of my journey.

The solace I found wasn't just in the formal rituals of church attendance or the structured support of the group meetings. It was also in the quiet moments of solitude, the moments when I could connect with God on a personal level. I found myself drawn to nature, spending hours walking in the woods, feeling the peace of the forest enveloping me. The stillness of the mornings, the quiet grandeur of the mountains, helped to center my thoughts, to quiet the incessant chatter of my mind, and to create space for prayer and reflection.

Prayer wasn't always easy. There were days when I felt a profound sense of emptiness, when my faith felt fragile and tenuous, when the words felt hollow and meaningless. But I persisted, even during the moments of doubt, because I realized that the act of prayer itself was an act of faith, a testament to my unwavering desire to connect with something larger than myself.

My newfound faith wasn't a panacea; it didn't magically erase my past or eradicate my struggles. The cravings still surfaced, sometimes with surprising intensity. The temptation to relapse, to escape the pain and the struggle, remained a constant challenge. But my faith provided me with the strength and resilience to resist those temptations, to weather those storms. It gave me a new framework, a new perspective on my life and my struggles. It offered a sense of purpose and meaning that had been previously absent.

The healing process was gradual, a slow, painstaking rebuilding of my life, one brick at a time. I started attending therapy sessions again, this time integrating my spiritual journey into the therapeutic process. My therapist, initially skeptical, came to appreciate the transformative power of my faith. He recognized that my spiritual awakening wasn't just a coping mechanism, but a genuine transformation that was driving my recovery and giving me a newfound sense of self-worth.

The process wasn't without its setbacks. There were moments when I felt overwhelmed by despair, when the weight of my past threatened to crush me. But each time, I found my way back to my faith, back to the support of my community, back to the quiet solace of prayer and reflection. My faith became a lifeline, a source of unwavering strength and guidance.

I began volunteering at a local homeless shelter, finding a sense of purpose and meaning in serving others. The act of giving back, of using my experiences to help those who were struggling, was immensely healing. It helped to shift my focus from my own struggles to the needs of others, reminding me that my experiences, though painful, had given me a unique perspective and the capacity to empathize with others' pain.

The transformation wasn't just spiritual; it was holistic. My newfound faith permeated every aspect of my life, impacting my relationships, my work, and my interactions with the world. I learned to forgive myself, to accept my imperfections, and to embrace the challenges of life with a newfound sense of courage and resilience.

The journey was far from over. The path to recovery is a lifelong journey, and there will undoubtedly be future challenges and setbacks. But the foundation of faith that I had built, the community that I had found, and the resilience that I had developed would sustain me through whatever came my way. The path ahead remained uncertain, but I knew, with a quiet confidence, that I was no longer walking it alone. I had God, my faith community, and the unwavering strength of my own spirit to guide me. The future held challenges, yes, but it also held the promise of continued healing, continued growth, and continued transformation – a transformation driven by faith, nurtured by love, and sustained by grace. The park, that crisp autumn afternoon, the kind stranger – these would forever be etched in my memory as the genesis of a new beginning, a testament to the enduring power of faith and the transformative grace of God.

The Power of Prayer and Meditation Finding Inner Peace

The solace I found in church, in the support group, and in the quietude of nature, deepened into a more intimate and personal practice: prayer and meditation. Initially, prayer felt stilted, forced. The words felt inadequate, clumsy attempts to articulate the turmoil within. I'd heard others speak of effortless communion with God, a feeling of profound connection and unwavering peace, and I felt like a fraud, a pretender struggling to mimic a spiritual grace I didn't possess. But I persisted, driven by a desperate need, a yearning for something beyond the chaos of my addiction-riddled past.

I started small, with simple, heartfelt requests. Not grand pronouncements or elaborate theological dissertations, but whispered pleas for strength, for guidance, for the courage to face another day without succumbing to the relentless pull of my addiction. I would kneel by my bed each morning, the worn wooden floorboards cold beneath my knees, and simply speak from the heart. Sometimes tears would stream down my face, a release of pent-up grief and remorse. Other times, a quiet peace would settle over me, a sense of calm amidst the storm.

The process wasn't always comfortable. My mind, long accustomed to the relentless chatter of addiction, struggled to find stillness. Thoughts would dart in and out, like restless spirits, disrupting the fragile peace I was attempting to cultivate. But I learned to gently redirect my thoughts, to acknowledge their presence without judgment, and to return my focus to my prayer. It was like training a wild animal, gently coaxing it back to its cage, rather than trying to force it into submission.

Meditation became a valuable companion to prayer. I started with guided meditations, finding solace in the calming voice of the instructor, the gentle rhythm of the breathing exercises. Gradually, I learned to meditate independently, finding my own rhythm, my own path to stillness. I would sit on a cushion by the window, watching the sunlight filter through the leaves, the gentle swaying branches mirroring the ebb and flow of my breath. Sometimes I would focus on my breath, the rising and falling of my chest, the gentle movement of the air in and out of my lungs. Other times, I would focus on a single point, a candle flame, a piece of artwork, allowing my mind to rest in the present moment, free from the anxieties of the past or the uncertainties of the future.

The practice of meditation helped me to develop a greater awareness of my emotions, my thoughts, my bodily sensations. I learned to recognize the subtle cues that signaled the approach of a craving, allowing me to take preventative measures before it spiralled into an uncontrollable urge. This self-awareness became an invaluable tool in my recovery. I learned to observe my cravings without judgment, acknowledging their presence without giving in to their demands. I would simply notice them, breathe through them, and allow them to pass.

The transformative power of prayer and meditation extended beyond the management of cravings. It helped me to cultivate a deeper sense of self-compassion and self-acceptance. For years, I had been consumed by self-loathing, by a relentless cycle of guilt and shame. Prayer and meditation helped me to break free from this cycle, to embrace my imperfections, and to forgive myself for the mistakes of my past.

It was during these quiet moments of prayer and meditation that I began to experience a profound sense of inner peace, a feeling of serenity that had eluded me for so long. This peace wasn't a constant state; it ebbed and flowed, like the tide. There were days when I felt overwhelmed by anxiety, by the weight of my past, by the challenges of the present. But the practice of prayer and meditation gave me the tools to navigate these difficult moments, to find solace amidst the storm. It gave me a refuge, a sanctuary where I could reconnect with my inner strength, my resilience, my faith.

The transformation was gradual, a slow and steady unfolding, like a flower blooming in the spring. It wasn't a sudden, dramatic shift, but a gradual evolution, a subtle shift in my perspective, my attitude, my way of being. I learned to appreciate the small things, the simple joys of life – the warmth of the sun on my skin, the beauty of a sunset, the laughter of a child. I learned to find gratitude in the midst of my struggles, to appreciate the blessings in my life, even when the challenges seemed overwhelming.

The stillness cultivated through prayer and meditation provided a fertile ground for introspection and self-discovery. It was in the quiet moments of solitude that I began to understand the root causes of my addiction, the wounds from my past that had driven me to seek solace in destructive behaviors. This understanding wasn't a simple revelation; it was a slow process of unwinding, a gradual peeling away of layers of denial, self-deception, and fear.

Prayer and meditation also fostered a deeper connection with my faith community. I began to see my fellow congregants not just as individuals, but as fellow travelers on a spiritual journey, each struggling with their own unique challenges, each seeking their own path to healing and redemption. This shared experience deepened the bonds of community, creating a sense of belonging, a sense of support that proved invaluable in my recovery.

The spiritual practices I adopted weren't simply tools for overcoming addiction; they were integral to a holistic healing process, influencing every aspect of my life. I found myself more patient with others, more understanding of their flaws and failings. My relationships became deeper, more authentic, more meaningful. My work became more fulfilling, my days more purposeful. I found a new joy in life, a new appreciation for its inherent beauty, its capacity for growth, its power to heal.

The path of faith, paved with prayer and meditation, wasn't always smooth or easy. There were moments of doubt, of despair, of questioning. There were times when I felt alone, abandoned, lost in the darkness. But through it all, the practices of prayer and meditation anchored me, provided a sense of grounding, a constant source of strength and resilience. They became my lifeline, my refuge, my path to inner peace. They remain so to this day. They are the quiet hum beneath the surface of my life, a constant reminder of the grace that sustains me, the love that surrounds me, and the peace that dwells within. The journey continues, but the foundation is solid, built on the unshakeable rock of faith, prayer, and the quiet, transformative power of meditation.

Connecting with a Community of Faith Finding Support and Belonging

The quiet solitude of prayer and meditation, while profoundly transformative, wasn't a solitary endeavor. My journey toward healing was inextricably linked to the embrace of a vibrant and supportive faith community. It wasn't simply attending services; it was the forging of genuine connections, the sharing of burdens, and the mutual encouragement that allowed my newfound faith to take root and flourish.

My first tentative steps into this community were marked by a deep sense of vulnerability. I remember the trembling in my hands as I approached the church for the first time after my release from rehab. The building itself, a simple brick structure nestled amongst towering oaks, felt both intimidating and comforting simultaneously. The air inside hummed with a quiet energy, a palpable sense of hope that contrasted sharply with the bleakness I'd carried for so long. I sat near the back, obscured by shadows, my gaze fixed on the worn wooden pews in front of me, my heart pounding in my chest.

The initial services were a blur of hymns and sermons. The words of the pastor, while deeply meaningful, often washed over me like a gentle wave. My focus was more on managing my own anxieties, the overwhelming fear that I might relapse, that I might somehow fail to live up to the expectations, both my own and those of the community. Yet, amidst the uncertainty, a quiet sense of peace began to settle over me. It wasn't a sudden transformation, but a gradual shift in my inner landscape. The sense of belonging I felt in these surroundings was unexpected; the presence of like-minded individuals, each striving for a life beyond their past struggles, was powerfully moving.

It was in the small groups that the true transformation began. These weren't large, impersonal gatherings. Instead, they consisted of a handful of individuals who met weekly to share their struggles, offer support, and pray together. The vulnerability within those small circles was profound. People shared stories of their own battles with addiction, their family struggles, their professional setbacks. There was no judgment, no condemnation, only empathy and understanding. The weight of my secrets, the burdens I'd carried in silence for so long, began to lift as I shared my story with others who truly understood.

One particular individual, a woman named Sarah, became a crucial part of my support network. Sarah had battled alcoholism for many years before finding sobriety through her faith. Her honesty and vulnerability were disarming; her story, filled with both heartache and hope, resonated deeply with my own experiences. She became a mentor, a confidante, a source of unwavering support during moments of doubt and despair. Her strength, her wisdom, and her unwavering faith served as a constant source of encouragement, a guiding light through my darkest hours.

Our meetings weren't always easy. There were times when raw emotion spilled forth, moments of intense grief, moments of anger and frustration. But within this safe space, these emotions were welcomed, acknowledged, and processed in a constructive way. We didn't shy away from the difficult realities of life; rather, we faced them together, drawing strength from the shared experience. We prayed together, not only for each other, but also for our families, our communities, and the world at large. These prayers weren't just rote recitations but heartfelt pleas born out of genuine need and a shared understanding.

Beyond the small group meetings, the church itself provided a sanctuary, a refuge from the anxieties of daily life. The simple act of attending services, singing hymns, listening to the sermon, became a vital part of my recovery process. The hymns, often filled with lyrics of hope, redemption, and perseverance, stirred something deep within me. They offered words of comfort, strength, and encouragement that helped to counter the negativity and self-doubt that I had carried for so long. The sermons often addressed themes of forgiveness, grace, and the transformative power of faith, which resonated deeply with my journey.

The church was more than just a building; it was a vibrant community. We participated in church picnics, fellowship dinners, and community service projects. These activities, seemingly simple and commonplace, served to further solidify my connection with the community. They provided opportunities for casual interactions, for building friendships, for fostering a sense of belonging. They were a refreshing counterpoint to the isolation I had experienced during my addiction. Through these interactions, I felt accepted, loved, and supported.

The support extended beyond the four walls of the church. Several members of the community offered practical assistance, helping me with things like transportation, childcare, and finding employment. This practical support was invaluable during the early stages of my recovery, relieving some of the burdens that could have easily overwhelmed me. It was a tangible manifestation of the love and compassion that radiated from this community of faith.

One particular instance stands out vividly in my mind. During a particularly challenging week, marked by intense cravings and self-doubt, I was on the verge of relapse. Overwhelmed by my emotions, I called Sarah, and she rushed over to my apartment. We sat and talked for hours, praying together, sharing tears, reminding one another of our shared faith and the strength we had discovered together. Her visit was a lifeline, preventing me from making a decision I would have deeply regretted. It was a powerful demonstration of the transformative power of genuine human connection, of the strength found in community.

The journey wasn't always easy. There were moments of doubt, moments of questioning, moments when I questioned my faith and my place within this community. But each time I faltered, I found support, encouragement, and understanding within the church family. I learned that setbacks are an inevitable part of the recovery process and that true healing is a journey, not a destination. The community provided a safe haven where I could stumble, pick myself up, and continue walking with the support of others who understood.

This sense of community wasn't merely a social network; it was a spiritual lifeline. It provided the framework for personal growth, allowing my faith to grow deeper and stronger, nourishing my spirit and providing a foundation for lasting recovery. The shared experience of faith, the mutual support, and the unwavering encouragement provided by this community was, and continues to be, an essential component of my ongoing journey toward a life of sobriety and spiritual growth. It is a constant reminder that we are not alone, that there is strength in community, and that even in the darkest moments, the light of faith can illuminate our path. The unwavering support of this community was the glue that held me together during the toughest times, proving that faith isn't just a belief system but a powerful force for healing and transformation.

Forgiveness and Acceptance Letting Go of the Past

The unwavering support of my church community wasn't just about fellowship and shared meals; it provided a crucial framework for confronting the deepest wounds of my past. My addiction wasn't just a physical dependence; it was a symptom of a deeper malaise, a self-loathing that had festered for years. The shame and guilt were crippling, heavy weights dragging me down, even after I'd achieved sobriety. It was within the context of my faith that I began to understand the power of forgiveness, both for myself and for others.

This understanding didn't dawn on me overnight. It was a gradual process, a slow unraveling of years of self-recrimination and bitterness. The initial steps were tentative, filled with doubt and uncertainty. I struggled to reconcile the image I had of myself – the broken, flawed individual consumed by addiction – with the image of the loving, forgiving God I was striving to believe in. The chasm between these two seemed insurmountable.

My journey towards self-forgiveness began with confession. Not just a simple acknowledgment of my mistakes, but a deep and heartfelt laying bare of my soul before God and, in time, before trusted members of my community. It was in the quiet stillness of my morning prayers, kneeling before my small altar in the corner of my apartment, that I began to articulate the depth of my regret, the weight of my actions. Tears flowed freely, not just tears of sorrow, but tears of release, a letting go of the burden I had carried for so long.

These prayers weren't always eloquent or well-formed. Sometimes they were just raw cries of anguish, desperate pleas for mercy and understanding. But within the quiet intimacy of these private moments, a sense of peace began to emerge. It wasn't a sudden erasure of my past, but a gradual softening of the harsh judgment I had imposed upon myself. God, in His infinite mercy, didn't condemn me for my failings. Instead, His love embraced me, offering a path toward healing and restoration.

The church building itself became a sanctuary, a place where I could find refuge from the relentless self-criticism. The stained-glass windows, casting vibrant colors onto the worn wooden pews, seemed to symbolize the beauty and grace that could emerge from even the darkest of times. The hymns, filled with themes of redemption and forgiveness, resonated deeply within me, offering words of comfort and hope that I desperately needed.

One particular hymn, "Amazing Grace," became a personal anthem. Its simple yet profound lyrics spoke directly to my heart, reminding me that God's grace was sufficient for even my deepest failings. The repeated refrain, "Amazing grace, how sweet the sound, that saved a wretch like me," became a mantra, a constant reminder of God's unwavering love and compassion. Singing along with the congregation, feeling the collective spirit of faith surrounding me, provided a powerful sense of solace and acceptance.

Beyond the formal services, the small group meetings proved to be invaluable in my journey toward self-forgiveness. Sharing my story with others who had experienced similar struggles was incredibly liberating. Hearing their stories of repentance, healing, and reconciliation helped me to realize that I wasn't alone in my struggles. Their experiences served as a powerful testament to the transformative power of faith and forgiveness.

The sharing wasn't always easy. There were moments of intense emotion, times when raw vulnerability threatened to overwhelm us. But within the safe and supportive environment of the small group, these emotions were met with compassion, empathy, and understanding. There was no judgment, no condemnation, only a shared understanding of the human experience. We didn't shy away from the hard truths; we faced them head-on, drawing strength from our shared struggles and our shared faith.

Forgiveness, however, wasn't solely about forgiving myself. It also involved forgiving others who had hurt me in the past. This proved to be a more challenging task, one that required a significant shift in my perspective. Holding onto resentment and anger only served to perpetuate the cycle of pain. Forgiving others wasn't about condoning their actions; it was about releasing the bitterness that had held me captive for so long.

My faith offered a framework for this process, reminding me that holding onto anger and resentment only harmed me. Jesus' teachings on forgiveness, exemplified in the parable of the unforgiving servant, resonated deeply within me. I realized that choosing to forgive wasn't just an act of grace toward others; it was an act of self-compassion, a way of freeing myself from the shackles of bitterness and resentment.

One specific instance stands out. There was a person from my past, someone who had significantly contributed to my descent into addiction. Holding onto the anger and resentment towards this individual was a constant source of pain. Through prayer and meditation, I gradually began to shift my perspective. I understood that forgiving this person wasn't about condoning their actions; it was about freeing myself from the weight of the negative emotions.

The act of forgiveness didn't erase the pain of the past. It didn't magically heal the wounds. It was more a decision, a conscious choice to release the anger and bitterness, to replace the negativity with compassion and understanding. The process was gradual, unfolding over time, and it required ongoing effort. However, the peace that followed was profound.

Forgiveness, both of myself and of others, didn't erase the past, but it changed my relationship to it. It allowed me to view my experiences with a new perspective, one that acknowledged the pain and suffering but didn't define me. It allowed me to move forward, to embrace the future with hope and optimism. It was a crucial step in my healing journey, a testament to the transformative power of faith and the enduring grace of God.

The acceptance that followed forgiveness was equally important. It was about acknowledging my past, both the good and the bad, without judgment or condemnation. It was about embracing my imperfections, recognizing that my mistakes didn't define who I was. It was about finding peace in the present, appreciating the blessings in my life, and looking forward to the future with hope.

This acceptance wasn't a passive resignation; it was an active choice. It was a conscious decision to embrace my whole self, flaws and all, and to view my life as a journey of growth and transformation. This journey wasn't linear; it had its ups and downs, its moments of triumph and setbacks. But within the context of my faith, I learned to view these experiences as opportunities for growth, as chances to learn and evolve.

The physical spaces where this transformation unfolded played a significant role. The quiet solitude of my apartment, where I poured out my heart in prayer, was a crucial sanctuary. The comforting embrace of the church building, with its stained-glass windows and hushed reverence, provided a powerful sense of peace and hope. The small group meetings, taking place in various homes, fostered a sense of intimacy and shared vulnerability.

Each location, in its own unique way, contributed to the overall process of healing and transformation. They weren't just physical spaces; they were sacred grounds, where faith and forgiveness intertwine, and where the burden of the past was gradually released, making way for the embrace of a more hopeful future. The journey wasn't easy, but the peace that followed was worth the effort, a testament to the enduring power of faith, forgiveness, and self-acceptance.

Entering Treatment Facing Challenges HeadOn

The car ride to the rehabilitation center felt like a journey into the unknown. My hands, usually clammy with anxiety, were surprisingly still, a strange calmness settling over me. This wasn't the surrender I had anticipated; it felt more like a deliberate step, a conscious choice to face my demons head-on. The years of denial and self-deception had finally given way to a desperate hope for something better. The facility itself, nestled amongst towering pines, was less imposing than I'd imagined. It wasn't a prison; it was a place of quiet resolve, a sanctuary for those seeking redemption.

Entering the building, I was struck by the air of quiet intensity. It wasn't a somber atmosphere, but a focused one, a place where every conversation, every shared glance, held a weight of shared experience. The staff, with their compassionate eyes and gentle smiles, welcomed me without judgment. They knew my story, my struggles, and yet, they saw beyond the addiction, recognizing the broken but resilient spirit within.

My initial days were a blur of assessments, orientations, and group therapy sessions. Each session was an opportunity to confront the root causes of my addiction, to unravel the tangled threads of my past. These weren't easy conversations. There were moments of intense vulnerability, where raw emotions threatened to overwhelm me. Yet, within the safe and structured environment of the facility, I felt a sense of belonging I had never known before.

Group therapy was particularly challenging. Sharing my story with complete strangers, exposing the darkest aspects of my past, felt terrifying initially. However, hearing the stories of others, recognizing the shared struggles and universal experiences of pain and loss, provided a powerful sense of solidarity. There was no need to downplay my experiences. Within this group, surrounded by people who understood, the shame and guilt I carried began to dissipate.

Individual therapy sessions provided a deeper dive into my past traumas, offering a chance to explore the psychological underpinnings of my addiction. My therapist, a wise and compassionate woman with years of experience, helped me to uncover the underlying issues – the emotional wounds that had fueled my self-destructive behaviors. This process wasn't easy; it required confronting difficult memories, acknowledging past hurts, and facing the consequences of my choices.

One particularly difficult session focused on my childhood. Memories I had suppressed for years flooded back, vivid and painful. The therapist guided me through the process with patience and understanding, helping me to process these memories in a healthy and constructive way. It was a profoundly emotional experience, but it was also incredibly liberating. For the first time, I began to understand the roots of my addiction, to see the connection between my past experiences and my present struggles.

The physical challenges of detox were immense. The withdrawal symptoms were excruciating, both physically and emotionally. There were days when I felt like giving up, days when the pain seemed unbearable. Yet, in those moments, my faith became my anchor, a source of unwavering strength. The prayers I offered, sometimes whispered, sometimes screamed in agony, sustained me.

I found solace in the simple routines of the facility. The daily walks along the nature trails provided moments of quiet contemplation. The structured schedule, with its clearly defined times for meals, therapy, and rest, provided a sense of order and stability. These routines provided a framework, a sense of normalcy amid the chaos of withdrawal. They were small victories, building blocks in the foundation of recovery.

The spiritual programs offered within the facility were invaluable. Daily meditation sessions provided moments of peace and reflection. Bible studies helped me to reconnect with the core tenets of my faith, reminding me of the unwavering love and forgiveness of God. These sessions weren't just religious exercises; they were opportunities to connect with my inner self, to find meaning and purpose in my struggle.

The other residents in the facility became my newfound family. We shared meals, stories, and struggles. We laughed together, cried together, and supported each other through the difficult moments. We created a community of mutual support, a network of shared experience, providing strength when we felt weak, encouragement when we felt discouraged. The bonds we formed transcended the confines of the rehabilitation center. They continued long after our individual journeys ended.

One resident, a kind older man named Michael, became a mentor. He'd been sober for twenty years, and he offered guidance and support that I needed during the challenging times. His story of redemption, of perseverance and unwavering faith, provided hope and inspiration. He shared his own struggles, demonstrating his vulnerabilities, making me feel less alone in my journey. His kindness, his empathy, became a beacon of hope amidst my struggles.

Week after week, I participated in therapy sessions, engaging in the introspective work required to unearth the underlying issues driving my addiction. I had to confront my past behaviors, acknowledge their consequences, and accept the responsibility for my actions. This process was painful, forcing me to confront long-buried emotions and memories. But it was also crucial for my long-term healing.

The end of my treatment program wasn't a sudden cure, a magical transformation. It was a stepping stone, a transition point, marking a shift in my perspective and a new direction in my life. I left the facility with a newfound sense of self-awareness, a deeper understanding of my struggles, and a commitment to ongoing recovery. The challenges continued even after I left, but I was better equipped to handle them, armed with the tools and support I had gained during my treatment.

The support network extended beyond the walls of the rehabilitation center. My church community remained steadfast in their support, providing encouragement, prayer, and practical assistance during the transition. Their consistent love and compassion was a significant factor in my successful transition back into society. It was a testament to the power of faith and community in the journey of recovery.

Looking back, the time spent at the rehabilitation center wasn't just about overcoming addiction; it was a journey of self-discovery, a path toward healing and wholeness. It was a time of confronting my deepest fears, acknowledging my flaws, and embracing my imperfections. It was a testament to the resilience of the human spirit, the power of faith, and the transformative potential of forgiveness, both of self and others. This was the beginning, not the end, of my journey.

Navigating Triggers and Cravings Maintaining Sobriety

Leaving the rehabilitation center wasn't a magical cure; it was a graduation into a new, more challenging phase of my recovery. The structured environment, the constant support, the predictable routines – all of that vanished the moment I stepped back into the world. Suddenly, I was faced with the stark reality of navigating my triggers and cravings without the safety net of the facility. The fear was palpable, a constant companion whispering doubts and anxieties in my ear. But I had learned valuable lessons during my time in treatment, and I was determined to apply them.

My first line of defense was prayer. It had been my lifeline during detox, and it remained so as I faced the challenges of everyday life. I didn't just pray for strength; I prayed for guidance, for discernment, for the wisdom to recognize and avoid situations that could lead to relapse. I learned to pray constantly, not just in formal settings but also in the quiet moments of the day – while waiting for a bus, while washing dishes, while walking my dog. These silent prayers became a rhythm, a pulse that kept me grounded. They weren't always eloquent or dramatic; often, they were simple pleas, desperate whispers for help. But they were always heard, always answered, in ways both big and small. Sometimes, the answer was a sudden shift in perspective, a moment of clarity that allowed me to see a situation differently. Other times, it was the unexpected appearance of a supportive friend, a timely intervention that pulled me back from the brink.

Meditation became another essential tool. The daily meditation sessions at the facility had instilled in me a practice I continued to cherish. It wasn't about clearing my mind entirely, but about focusing on the present moment, on the breath flowing in and out of my body. During cravings, I would find a quiet space, close my eyes, and concentrate on my breath. The simple act of focusing on my breath helped to ground me, to anchor me in the present, preventing my mind from wandering into the dangerous territory of rumination and self-doubt. It helped to separate me from the overwhelming tide of cravings and to regain a sense of control. It helped me to remember that these intense feelings were temporary, that they would pass.

My faith community played a vital role in my recovery. The unwavering support of my church family had been a source of strength throughout my treatment, and it continued to be so as I navigated the challenges of life outside the facility. I was no longer simply attending services; I was actively engaging with the community, participating in small groups, and offering my assistance wherever I could. This active participation wasn't just about receiving support; it was also about giving back, about contributing to something larger than myself. It helped me to focus on the positive aspects of life, to replace the self-centeredness of addiction with a sense of purpose and belonging. The friendships I formed within the church were a lifeline, offering comfort, encouragement, and accountability. My church friends understood my struggles, they celebrated my victories, and they helped me to remain grounded in my faith. There were times when the temptation to slip was overwhelming; then, a phone call, a text, or a visit from a church member was enough to remind me of the support system I had cultivated. Their presence, their prayers, and their encouragement were instrumental in preventing relapse.

Certain places triggered intense cravings. The bar where I had spent countless nights, the park where I had first used, even the grocery store where I had bought alcohol – these places became emotionally charged territory. Initially, I avoided these places entirely, understanding the profound emotional and physical connection I had built with them. However, complete avoidance wasn't a sustainable long-term solution. The world couldn't be avoided. So, I developed strategies to approach them with increased awareness and safety. I didn't avoid them completely, but I planned my route, ensuring a trusted friend would accompany me. I rehearsed positive self-talk, mentally reminding myself of my reasons for sobriety. I also visualized myself walking through the space, confident and resolute, not succumbing to the pressure. This mental preparation was surprisingly effective. It reduced the intensity of my anxiety, making these places less daunting.

My approach to cravings evolved over time. In the early stages of recovery, cravings were intense and almost unbearable. I relied heavily on prayer, meditation, and my support system to navigate these difficult moments. I learned to identify my triggers and to develop coping mechanisms. I kept a journal, documenting my cravings, the situations that triggered them, and the strategies I used to manage them. This self-reflection helped me to identify patterns and to refine my approach. Over time, the intensity of my cravings diminished, though they never disappeared completely. They became more manageable, less overwhelming, more like ripples in a calm sea than the crashing waves of my early recovery. This journal became a chronicle of my progress, a testament to my perseverance. It helped to break down large challenges into small, measurable victories.

The temptation to relapse never truly goes away. Even years into my recovery, there are moments when I'm tempted to return to my old ways. But my faith, my support system, and the tools I learned in rehabilitation equip me to face these challenges. I continue to pray regularly, to meditate daily, and to actively engage with my faith community. I remain vigilant about my triggers and proactively avoid situations that could put me at risk. I use coping mechanisms I've developed – exercise, creative activities, spending time in nature – to manage my cravings and to maintain a healthy, balanced life. My recovery isn't a linear progression; it's a winding road with ups and downs, challenges and victories. But with faith as my guiding light and my community as my support, I remain committed to my journey of sobriety. It's a testament to the power of God's grace and the transformative potential of recovery.

Maintaining sobriety is an ongoing journey, not a destination. Each day presents new challenges, new temptations, and new opportunities for growth. But through faith, prayer, meditation, and the unwavering support of my community, I continue to navigate these challenges with strength and resilience. The struggles are real, the temptations are constant, but so is the unwavering support of my faith, my community, and my inner resolve. My journey is a testament to the enduring power of hope, the transformative nature of faith, and the boundless grace of God. The road is long, but with each step forward, I am more confident in my ability to remain sober and to live a life filled with purpose and meaning. The experiences I've shared aren't just mine; they're a reflection of the universal struggle, the shared human experience of overcoming adversity and finding redemption through faith. This ongoing journey reinforces the importance of self-compassion, perseverance, and continued reliance on the support network that surrounds me. My story is one of continuous growth, of adapting and evolving as I navigate the complexities of life in sobriety. This ongoing journey teaches me to embrace imperfection, to find strength in vulnerability, and to always seek guidance from a higher power. The peace I've found is not an absence of challenges, but a quiet strength found amidst the storms of life. It's a continuous journey of faith, resilience, and the unwavering belief in the possibility of a better tomorrow. And that's a journey worth sharing.

Building Healthy Habits Reclaiming Control of Life

Leaving the rehabilitation center was like stepping off a life raft onto a turbulent sea. The structured safety of the program was gone, replaced by the unpredictable currents of daily life. My carefully constructed foundation of prayer, meditation, and community support needed to become my own, personally tailored, and self-sustained lifeboat. This required building a new life, brick by brick, habit by habit, relying on my newfound faith to guide my actions.

My home, once a place of despair and isolation, was now the heart of my recovery. I transformed it into a sanctuary, a space of peace and intention. I started small, decluttering and cleaning, a physical act that mirrored the mental and emotional cleansing I was undergoing. Every discarded object represented a piece of my past, a symbol of the chaos and dysfunction I was actively leaving behind. The process was cathartic, liberating. As I cleared the physical space, I felt a corresponding sense of clarity and lightness in my mind and soul.

I established a daily routine, a schedule as rigorous as my treatment plan, but designed for self-governance rather than external enforcement. My mornings began with prayer and meditation, a quiet time of reflection and communion with God. I chose passages from scripture that resonated with my present needs, passages that offered hope, strength, and guidance. Sometimes, I would simply sit in silence, allowing the peace of God to settle over me. I learned to listen to the quiet whispers of my spirit, to discern the guidance offered in the stillness.

The gym became my physical sanctuary. Exercise was more than just a way to stay healthy; it was a powerful tool for managing my cravings and stress. The physical exertion helped to release endorphins, creating a natural high that quelled the urge for chemical stimulation. The structured repetition of the workouts provided a sense of discipline and order, counteracting the impulsive nature of my addiction. More than this, it was a commitment, a promise kept to myself, a visible symbol of the dedication to my recovery.

Evenings were reserved for quiet reflection. This wasn't always easy. The stillness could be overwhelming, allowing the insidious whispers of doubt and self-criticism to creep in. But I persevered, learning to recognize these thoughts for what they were—lies, whispers from the enemy, designed to undermine my progress. I learned to replace them with affirmations of God's love and grace, reminding myself of my worth and my potential for healing. I'd read inspirational literature, the words reinforcing the path I had chosen. It helped fill the void that once craved substances.

Developing these habits wasn't easy. There were days when fatigue overwhelmed me, days when the cravings were intense, and days when I felt overwhelmed by the enormity of the task. But I remembered the lessons from rehab. I'd write about my struggles, not just as a way to vent but as an opportunity to examine my patterns, identify my triggers, and discover new coping mechanisms. My journal became a testament to my struggle and a chronicle of my progress, each entry a milestone on my road to recovery. I learned to celebrate small victories, to recognize that every moment of sobriety was a significant achievement.

My faith was, and continues to be, my anchor in the storms of recovery. It wasn't just a passive belief; it was an active participation in a loving community, a source of unwavering support. My church family was more than a congregation; it was my extended family, my lifeline. The shared experiences, the collective prayers, the unwavering encouragement—these were essential components to my journey. I attended services regularly, actively engaging in small groups, and volunteering my time whenever possible. The act of giving back, of serving others, was a powerful antidote to the self-centeredness of addiction.

One particular event solidified this sense of community. During a particularly challenging week, when the temptation to relapse felt overwhelming, a member of my church family noticed my struggle. They called, not with judgment but with genuine concern, offering practical assistance and unwavering support. They simply listened, offering prayer and empathy. This act of compassion was more powerful than any sermon, any inspirational quote. It was a tangible demonstration of God's love, a reminder that I was not alone in my struggle.

The structure I had created in my life wasn't static; it evolved with my changing needs. My routine wasn't about rigid adherence to a schedule but about creating a framework that provided stability and predictability in the midst of life's inevitable chaos. As my sobriety progressed, I gradually introduced new activities that nourished my soul and strengthened my resolve. I took up painting, finding solace and creativity in the act of self-expression. I developed a passion for gardening, appreciating the connection between growth and nurturing.

I found quiet moments in nature, finding peace and perspective amidst the serenity of God's creation. These activities weren't just hobbies; they were therapeutic tools, alternative channels for expression and self-soothing that helped to divert my focus away from the destructive impulses that had once dictated my life.

The journey wasn't linear. There were setbacks, moments of weakness, and the occasional near-miss. But with each stumble, I learned to get back up, to dust myself off, and to continue forward with renewed determination. My faith, my community, and the healthy habits I had cultivated were my safety net, catching me and preventing me from falling too far. The imperfections became lessons, shaping my path and strengthening my resolve. The setbacks were not failures, but opportunities for growth and learning, refining my understanding of myself and my needs.

My recovery became a testament to the transformative power of faith, the importance of community, and the life-affirming strength of healthy habits. It was a process of reclaiming control over my life, one day, one hour, one minute at a time. It was a journey marked not just by the absence of addiction but by the presence of faith, purpose, and a life brimming with love, joy, and peace. The transformation wasn't sudden; it was gradual, almost imperceptible at times, but undeniable in its impact. The change wasn't just about physical and mental healing; it was a profound spiritual transformation, a rebirth, a testament to the enduring power of God's grace and the unwavering resilience of the human spirit. My journey continues, and with every passing day, I am more grateful for the gift of sobriety, the strength to persevere, and the faith that sustains me.

Rebuilding Relationships Repairing Broken Bonds

The quiet hum of the church organ was a comforting backdrop as I sat, nervously clutching a worn copy of the Psalms. Today was the day. Today, I was going to face my family. The chasm between us felt vast, an impassable canyon carved by years of lies, broken promises, and the devastating consequences of my addiction. My mother, in particular, had borne the brunt of my self-destruction. Her silent suffering had been a heavy weight on my conscience, a constant reminder of the pain I had inflicted.

The church wasn't just a place of worship; it had become my refuge, a sanctuary where I could connect with God and find the strength to navigate the treacherous terrain of rebuilding my life. It was here, surrounded by the supportive community I had found, that I'd gained the courage to attempt the impossible: to mend the fractured relationships that addiction had shattered.

My hands trembled as I dialed my mother's number. The ringing tone echoed the frantic beat of my heart. When she answered, her voice was hesitant, cautious, laced with a guardedness that mirrored my own apprehension. The conversation was stilted at first, filled with awkward silences and hesitant words. Years of unspoken resentments and unhealed wounds lay between us, a formidable obstacle to overcome.

But slowly, miraculously, the ice began to thaw. I spoke from the heart, expressing my deepest remorse for the pain I had caused, admitting the depth of my failings without excuses or justifications. It wasn't easy. The words choked me, the weight of my guilt almost unbearable. Yet, with each confession, with each expression of sorrow, a sense of release washed over me. My mother listened patiently, her initial reserve gradually melting away as my sincerity became evident.

The meeting itself was a revelation. We met at a small café near her house, a neutral territory that felt both safe and vulnerable. The aroma of freshly brewed coffee did little to mask the emotional intensity of our reunion. As we talked, memories flooded back: happy childhood moments interwoven with the painful reality of my descent into addiction. Tears flowed freely, tears of sorrow, remorse, and – surprisingly – of hope. For the first time in a long time, I saw a flicker of forgiveness in my mother's eyes.

That first meeting was just the beginning. Reconciliation didn't happen overnight; it was a gradual process, a delicate dance of forgiveness and acceptance. We started small, meeting regularly for coffee, sharing mundane details of our daily lives, slowly rebuilding the bonds of trust that had been broken. We started with short visits, then longer ones, until the distance between us shrunk, and the gulf that had separated us narrowed to a manageable stream. I began to see her not as my accuser, but as a woman who had endured unimaginable pain, her love for me unwavering despite my failures.

My relationship with my father was different. He had always been more reserved, his emotions less outwardly expressed. He didn't express his hurt as openly as my mother, but the silence spoke volumes. Our reconciliation was less emotional, more pragmatic. We started by working together on small projects around his house, a shared activity that allowed us to connect without the pressure of intense emotional confrontations. The quiet hum of the lawnmower, the rhythmic thud of the hammer, became the soundtrack to our slow, steady reconciliation. We didn't discuss my past explicitly, but the shared work, the silent presence, spoke of acceptance, of a gradual rebuilding of our relationship.

My siblings presented their own challenges. Some were more understanding than others, their reactions colored by their own experiences and personalities. With some, the process was quick, a simple phone call or a heartfelt letter clearing the air. With others, it was a more arduous journey, requiring patience, persistence, and a willingness to listen without defensiveness. My faith guided me through these interactions. The scripture, "Forgive us our debts, as we also have forgiven our debtors" became my guiding principle.

Beyond my immediate family, there were friends to reconnect with. Some had distanced themselves, hurt and disappointed by my actions. Others remained supportive, their loyalty a testament to the strength of our bonds. Reapproach these individuals demanded humility. I reached out, not with expectation, but with a sincere desire to apologize and begin the process of amends. It was humbling to acknowledge the pain I had inflicted, to accept their anger and disappointment without bitterness.

One friend, a childhood companion named Sarah, was particularly challenging. Our friendship had been deeply significant, and her hurt was palpable. Our first conversation was fraught with tension. I listened patiently as she voiced her disappointment, her anger. There were tears, accusations, and moments of silence that felt heavy with unspoken pain. But through it all, I held onto my faith, my belief in forgiveness and the transformative power of grace. Slowly, tentatively, we began to rebuild our friendship, acknowledging the past but focusing on the future. It wasn't the same as before, but it was a new kind of friendship, stronger and more meaningful because of what we had overcome.

The road to rebuilding relationships was long and arduous, filled with setbacks and moments of doubt. There were times when I wanted to give up, when the weight of my past felt too heavy to bear. But my faith provided the strength and perseverance I needed. Through prayer, meditation, and the unwavering support of my church community, I found the courage to keep going, to keep striving for reconciliation and healing. The process taught me the importance of humility, forgiveness, and the transformative power of grace. It was a journey that reaffirmed my belief in the restorative nature of love, faith, and the resilience of the human spirit. The scars of the past would remain, but they would be reminders of the grace that had transformed my life and mended the broken bonds I held dear. The love and acceptance I received, not just from God, but from those I had hurt, was a constant source of strength and hope, demonstrating the healing power of genuine repentance and the enduring strength of the human spirit. It was, and continues to be, a journey of faith, forgiveness, and the slow, painstaking reconstruction of a life and relationships once irrevocably shattered.

Forgiving Myself Embracing SelfCompassion

The reconciliation with my family was a monumental step, but the true depth of my recovery lay in forgiving myself. This wasn't a simple act; it was a continuous process, a daily wrestling match with the ghosts of my past. For years, I'd carried the weight of my actions like a leaden cloak, suffocating me with self-recrimination. The shame was a constant companion, whispering insidious doubts and accusations in the quiet hours of the night. I judged myself harshly, replaying past mistakes in a relentless loop of self-flagellation. I couldn't escape the feeling that I was irredeemably flawed, unworthy of love, undeserving of forgiveness.

This internal battle took place in many settings – in the quiet solitude of my small apartment, amidst the bustling energy of the city streets, and most profoundly, within the sanctuary of the church. The church wasn't just a physical building; it was a spiritual haven, a place where I could connect with God and receive the grace that I so desperately craved. In the hushed reverence of the sanctuary, I learned the importance of self-compassion, a concept that initially felt foreign and even hypocritical. How could I show compassion to myself after all the harm I had inflicted?

The answer, I discovered, lay in understanding the nature of grace. God's love, I came to believe, wasn't conditional; it wasn't dependent on my worthiness or my past actions. It was an unconditional gift, freely offered, freely received. This realization gradually shifted my perspective. I began to see myself not as an irredeemable sinner, but as a flawed human being, capable of both great darkness and immense potential for growth and healing. This understanding became the cornerstone of my self-forgiveness.

My faith provided a framework for self-compassion. The Bible's stories are replete with flawed individuals, people who made terrible mistakes yet found redemption. David's adultery and murder, Peter's denial of Christ – these weren't glossed over; they were central to their narratives. Yet, they were forgiven, embraced, and ultimately used by God to fulfill His divine purpose. These stories gave me hope, demonstrating that even the most grievous sins could be overcome through repentance and God's unwavering love.

The process wasn't linear; it was a journey filled with setbacks and relapses. There were days when the weight of my past felt unbearable, when the whispers of self-doubt threatened to overwhelm me. On those days, I found solace in prayer, pouring out my heart to God, acknowledging my failings, and seeking His strength and guidance. Meditation became another vital tool, providing a space for introspection and self-reflection. In the quiet stillness, I learned to observe my thoughts and emotions without judgment, allowing myself to feel the pain and sadness without getting lost in it. I learned to treat myself with the same kindness and understanding that I would offer a friend struggling with similar challenges.

Joining a support group within the church proved invaluable. Sharing my struggles with others who understood my pain, who had walked a similar path, created a powerful sense of community and mutual support. Hearing their stories, their struggles, and their triumphs, helped me realize that I wasn't alone in my journey. The shared experiences created a sense of solidarity, a feeling of belonging that countered the isolation and shame that had previously defined my existence. I learned that vulnerability was a strength, not a weakness.

Self-forgiveness didn't mean condoning my past actions; it meant accepting them as part of my story, a part that shaped me into the person I am today. It meant acknowledging the pain I had caused without dwelling on it endlessly. It meant releasing the grip of self-hatred and embracing the possibility of a new beginning, a life filled with purpose and meaning. This was a continuous process, a daily practice of self-compassion, a commitment to treat myself with the same kindness and grace that I had received from God and from others.

The physical environment also played a role. Spending time in nature, hiking in the nearby mountains, or simply sitting by the lake, helped to center me, to connect with something larger than myself. The vastness of the natural world put my problems in perspective, reminding me of the resilience of life and the power of renewal. Simple acts of self-care – healthy eating, regular exercise, and sufficient sleep – also became essential components of my journey. These weren't just physical acts; they were expressions of self-respect and a commitment to my well-being.

Beyond the physical and spiritual realms, there was the intellectual aspect of my recovery. I immersed myself in literature, seeking out stories of redemption and transformation. I devoured books on psychology, learning about the mechanisms of addiction and the pathways to healing. This intellectual engagement was a way of understanding my past, of making sense of the choices I had made. It helped me to see my addiction not as a moral failing, but as a complex illness requiring treatment and understanding.

Reading the writings of other recovering addicts proved particularly helpful. Their stories resonated deeply with me, providing validation and hope. These weren't just tales of woe; they were narratives of resilience, of transformation, of the incredible capacity of the human spirit to overcome adversity. Their honesty and vulnerability were powerful reminders that I was not alone in my journey, that others had struggled, faltered, and ultimately found their way back to a life of purpose and meaning.

Forgiving myself wasn't a single act of forgiveness but a continuous process of letting go of self-judgment and embracing self-compassion. It was a journey that took me through dark valleys and brought me to sunlit peaks. It was a journey that required perseverance, faith, and a relentless commitment to self-love. It involved not only confronting the painful realities of my past but also actively cultivating self-compassion in the present. This involved practicing mindfulness to become more aware of my self-criticism and actively challenging those negative thoughts. I learned to replace self-deprecating statements with encouraging and supportive affirmations.

Furthermore, I actively sought out opportunities to practice self-compassion. When confronted with setbacks, I treated myself with the same kindness and understanding that I would offer a friend. I acknowledged my struggles without judgment, recognizing that imperfections are part of the human experience. I celebrated my small victories, appreciating my progress along the way, rather than dwelling on the areas where I still needed growth. This positive reinforcement helped to build a sense of self-worth and resilience.

My journey of self-forgiveness was deeply intertwined with my faith. My belief in God's unwavering love provided the foundation for self-acceptance. Through prayer, meditation, and active participation in my church community, I found the strength and guidance to navigate the challenges of healing. My faith reminded me that I am a child of God, inherently worthy of love and forgiveness, despite my imperfections. This belief empowered me to approach myself with compassion, recognizing my inherent worth as a human being.

In conclusion, the path to self-forgiveness is a long, winding road, requiring consistent effort and self-reflection. It is a journey that demands both courage and vulnerability. But with the unwavering support of faith, community, and a dedication to self-compassion, it is a journey that is possible to undertake and ultimately, to complete. The scars may remain, but they become a testament to the strength and resilience of the human spirit, a reminder of the transformative power of grace, both received and given to oneself. The quiet hum of self-acceptance is a far more profound and lasting melody than the cacophony of self-recrimination that once dominated my life.

Finding My Calling Pursuing a Life of Meaning

The quiet hum of self-acceptance, a melody replacing the cacophony of self-recrimination, opened a space for something new to emerge: purpose. Forgiveness, both of myself and others, hadn't just healed old wounds; it had cleared a path, revealing possibilities I hadn't dared to imagine before. The question wasn't just *how* to live, but *why*. My past, once a weight crushing me to the earth, now felt like a foundation, solid and strong, upon which I could build a new life, one filled with meaning and contribution.

This wasn't a sudden epiphany, a bolt of lightning illuminating my path. It was a gradual dawning, a slow unfolding of awareness. It began subtly, with small acts of kindness, gestures that extended beyond myself. Helping an elderly neighbor with groceries, volunteering at a local soup kitchen, offering a listening ear to a friend struggling with their own demons—these weren't grand gestures, but they were significant nonetheless. They were small acts of service, fueled by a newfound sense of empathy and compassion, a desire to give back to the community that had shown me such grace.

My faith played an integral role in this process. The scriptures are replete with stories of individuals who used their experiences, their pain, their struggles, to serve God and others. I began to see my own past, my addiction, not as a shameful secret to be hidden away, but as a testament to God's grace and a source of strength and wisdom. My struggles had shaped me, honed my empathy, and equipped me with a unique perspective that I could now use to help others.

The transition wasn't always smooth. Doubt still crept in, whispering insidious suggestions that I wasn't capable, that I wasn't worthy. There were moments of self-doubt, times when the old patterns of self-recrimination threatened to resurface. But the difference was this: I now possessed the tools to combat these negative thoughts. I had developed strategies to manage my inner critic, employing techniques learned through meditation, prayer, and therapy. I had established healthy coping mechanisms that allowed me to manage stress and avoid unhealthy behaviors. I had built a support network that provided encouragement and accountability.

One day, while volunteering at a local homeless shelter, a young man approached me, his eyes filled with despair. He reminded me of myself years ago, lost and alone, desperate for a lifeline. In that moment, I recognized my calling. My experiences, my pain, my struggle, weren't just mine to bear; they were gifts, tools I could use to help others navigate their own dark nights. I realized that helping others wasn't just an act of service; it was an act of self-healing, a way of making amends for the past while also building a positive future.

This understanding led me to pursue a career in addiction counseling. The decision wasn't without apprehension. I had spent years battling my own demons; the thought of confronting them again, but this time in the context of supporting others, filled me with a mixture of excitement and trepidation. The process of becoming a certified counselor was rigorous, demanding long hours of study, clinical practice, and self-reflection. It required me to confront my own past traumas and biases, to examine the roots of my addiction, and to develop strategies for helping others to achieve recovery.

The classroom became a crucible, testing my resolve, pushing my limits, demanding more of me than I ever thought possible. The curriculum was comprehensive, delving into the intricacies of addiction, the complexities of trauma-informed care, and the nuances of effective therapeutic interventions. It was challenging, both academically and emotionally. There were times when the weight of it all became overwhelming, when the memories of my past threatened to engulf me. But I persevered, fueled by a desire to help others, by a belief in my own capacity for growth and change, and by the unwavering support of my faith.

The clinical setting presented a different type of challenge. The experience of working with clients struggling with similar challenges to my own was profoundly humbling. Their stories resonated with me on a deep emotional level; their vulnerability evoked a sense of compassion and empathy that was at once familiar and intensely powerful. This wasn't merely intellectual work; it was deeply personal and emotionally charged. Each client's journey became a reflection of my own. I felt immense responsibility to offer them not just clinical guidance, but also a sense of hope, connection, and belief in their ability to heal.

The success stories became profound moments of affirmation. Witnessing individuals overcome addiction, reclaim their lives, and find a renewed sense of purpose was an incredibly rewarding experience. It validated the challenges I had faced, the sacrifices I had made, and the path I had chosen to follow. Their journeys reflected my own, echoing the triumphs and struggles, the setbacks and comebacks, that are integral to the recovery process.

Simultaneously, I became deeply involved in my church community. I volunteered to lead a support group for recovering addicts, sharing my story openly and honestly, creating a safe and supportive environment for others to share their struggles. The group became a source of mutual support, a place of shared vulnerability and collective healing. My faith continued to be my anchor, providing strength, guidance, and solace during challenging times. The church wasn't just a place of worship; it was a vibrant community, a haven of support, a source of inspiration and purpose.

My work in addiction counseling continues to evolve, my understanding deepening with each client I encounter. I have learned to leverage both my personal experiences and my professional training, integrating my faith and understanding of addiction into a holistic approach to recovery. This path hasn't eliminated all challenges. There are days when exhaustion weighs heavily, when the emotional toll of the work feels almost unbearable. But the rewards outweigh the difficulties, a hundredfold.

I have discovered that my calling isn't just a career, but a calling from God, a confirmation of my worth and a testimony to the transforming power of His love. It's a path that allows me to combine my past experiences, my faith, and my professional skills to create positive change in the lives of others. The life of meaning I've found isn't defined by worldly achievements, but by the quiet satisfaction of knowing that I am living a life of purpose, a life dedicated to helping others find their own path to healing and redemption. The journey continues, but I am walking it with a renewed sense of hope, a deep-seated faith, and the unwavering knowledge that my past, though painful, has paved the way for my present purpose. This is the beautiful paradox of recovery: the pain transforms into purpose, the darkness reveals the light, and the scars become a testament to the enduring strength of the human spirit.

Giving Back to the Community Spreading Hope and Inspiration

The transition from recovering addict to addiction counselor wasn't merely a career change; it was a spiritual metamorphosis. My newfound purpose wasn't solely about personal redemption; it was about extending the grace and mercy I'd received to others grappling with similar demons. The initial steps were tentative, almost hesitant. Volunteering at the local homeless shelter felt like stepping into a minefield of memories, a landscape riddled with the ghosts of my own past. Yet, each interaction, each shared story, each act of compassion, served as an antidote to the lingering poison of self-doubt.

I remember one particular evening vividly. A young woman, no older than twenty, approached me, her eyes brimming with unshed tears. She recounted a story of abuse, neglect, and a desperate attempt to numb the pain with drugs. Her narrative was a mirror reflecting my own fractured past, highlighting the shared pain of addiction. It was in that moment, listening to her whispered confession, that the weight of my past truly began to lift. It was no longer a burden I carried alone; it was a shared experience, a bond forged in the crucible of shared trauma. In helping her, I was not only helping her; I was simultaneously healing myself.

My involvement with the shelter extended beyond offering a listening ear. I began to organize workshops on coping mechanisms, leading sessions on stress management, and sharing practical strategies for navigating cravings and triggers. I found a peculiar kind of solace in this work – a sense of making amends, of turning the pain of my past into a force for good. The energy and effort involved were significant; the emotional toll substantial. Yet, witnessing the subtle shifts in my clients, their growing confidence, their increasing self-worth, far outweighed any fatigue. It was a testament to the restorative power of empathy and compassion.

My participation in the local church community deepened concurrently with my work at the shelter. Initially, my role was primarily focused on lending a listening ear or offering support during coffee hour. However, as my confidence grew, I felt a profound calling to share my story publicly. The initial vulnerability was terrifying, a confrontation with my deepest fears. The shame and guilt, ghosts from the past, threatened to reemerge. But the support of my faith community, the understanding glances, the encouraging nods, gave me the courage to speak my truth.

I began by leading a small Bible study group focused on the themes of forgiveness, redemption, and healing. The vulnerability inherent in sharing my past transgressions was met with compassion and understanding. The group became a refuge, a sacred space where we could confront our struggles openly and honestly, offering each other support, encouragement, and unconditional love. The collective strength fostered within this community helped us navigate our respective challenges.

My sharing wasn't limited to small, intimate gatherings. I started to speak at larger church events, sharing my testimony with larger congregations. The nervousness was always present, a familiar knot tightening in my stomach. But the overwhelming sense of purpose overshadowed the fear. Each story shared, each shared tear, each moment of connection helped solidify my belief in the transformative power of faith.

The responses to my sharing were deeply moving. People approached me after services, sharing their own struggles, their own battles with addiction, and their own journeys to recovery. These conversations became testaments to the universality of human pain and the power of shared experience. My role became more than just sharing my story; it evolved into providing mentorship, guidance, and hope. It transformed into actively building a community of support for those still battling their addictions.

Beyond the church, I sought opportunities to expand my reach. I joined forces with local organizations dedicated to addiction recovery, volunteering my time and expertise to develop and implement outreach programs. We organized awareness campaigns, conducted workshops in schools, and facilitated support groups for families affected by addiction. The scope of the work was vast, encompassing a wide range of activities, from fundraising events to public speaking engagements. It was exhausting, but deeply fulfilling.

Working alongside other advocates for recovery broadened my perspective, challenging my preconceived notions and helping me refine my approach to helping others. I learned the value of collaboration, the significance of community support, and the importance of creating a multifaceted approach to recovery. The challenges were numerous, ranging from securing funding to navigating bureaucratic hurdles. Yet, the consistent affirmation that we were making a tangible difference kept us motivated.

The impact of our work was palpable. We witnessed families reunited, lives restored, and communities strengthened. We celebrated small victories, marking milestones in recovery, and commiserated over setbacks. We learned the profound importance of celebrating the small steps forward, understanding that recovery is not a linear progression, but a journey characterized by both triumphs and failures.

Through this collaborative work, I began developing a deeper understanding of the systemic factors that contribute to addiction. I recognized the limitations of individual solutions and the importance of addressing social and economic inequalities that fuel the cycle of addiction. This realization led me to advocate for policy changes that promote prevention and support recovery efforts. This advocacy, though challenging, aligned with my newfound understanding that true recovery encompassed both personal transformation and societal change.

My journey has been a testament to the power of redemption, a journey fueled by faith, strengthened by community, and validated by the transformative power of giving back. The challenges remain substantial, the work is never ending, but the rewards are immeasurable. The quiet hum of purpose, once a distant melody, now resonates within me, a constant reminder of the transformative power of using my past to create a brighter future for others. And in that giving, in that act of selfless service, I discovered not only my purpose, but also a profound and enduring sense of peace. This is my testimony, a testament to God's grace, to the enduring power of faith, and to the profound beauty of redemption found in the act of helping others find their way back to the light.

Building Strong Relationships Nurturing Healthy Connections

The sanctuary of my local church wasn't just a building; it became a haven, a place where fractured souls found solace and fractured lives began to mend. The familiar scent of old wood and beeswax, the comforting hymns, the shared silence during prayer – these were the tangible expressions of a community that embraced me, flaws and all. It wasn't a perfect community; disagreements arose, misunderstandings occurred, and imperfections were evident. But the underlying current of compassion, forgiveness, and unwavering support was undeniable.

My relationships within the church extended beyond the Sunday services. I formed deep connections with individuals who understood the unique challenges of recovery. There was Martha, a woman whose gentle wisdom and unwavering faith provided a steady anchor in my turbulent emotional seas. She had her own battles, her own scars, but her strength and resilience were an inspiration. We spent countless hours together, sharing stories, offering encouragement, and simply being present for one another. Our bond transcended age and circumstance; it was a sisterhood forged in the fires of shared adversity and strengthened by a shared faith.

Then there was Pastor John, a man whose compassionate heart and unwavering belief in redemption helped to solidify my own faith. His guidance wasn't preachy; it was practical, empathetic, and infused with a profound understanding of human frailty. He provided mentorship, not only in my spiritual journey but also in my professional development as an addiction counselor. He challenged me to grow, to step outside my comfort zone, and to embrace the opportunities to serve others. His quiet strength and unwavering belief in my potential were instrumental in my transformation.

My relationships outside the church were equally significant. The volunteers at the homeless shelter became an extended family. We shared laughter, tears, and a common commitment to helping those in need. The bond we forged was based on shared experiences, mutual respect, and a shared desire to make a difference. We celebrated each small victory, commiserated over setbacks, and provided unwavering support to each other during challenging times. Their unwavering commitment was a constant source of encouragement and inspiration. I wasn't just working alongside them; I was building friendships that would endure long after my formal volunteer work was done.

One particular friendship stood out – that of Daniel, a recovering addict who became both a colleague and a dear friend. Our shared past allowed for a level of understanding and empathy that transcended the usual professional boundaries. We could speak openly and honestly about our struggles, sharing our vulnerabilities without judgment. We supported each other's triumphs and commiserated over setbacks. His journey, parallel to my own, reminded me that recovery is a continuous process, a lifelong commitment. His presence became a constant source of support and a reminder that I was not alone.

The importance of these relationships cannot be overstated. They provided a safety net, a support system, a sense of belonging in a world that had once felt isolating and hostile. They filled the void left by the destructive relationships of my past, offering unconditional love, unwavering support, and a sense of community that sustained me through difficult times. They were a testament to the power of human connection and the importance of building healthy, supportive relationships.

My faith played a pivotal role in nurturing these connections. It provided a common ground, a shared belief system that fostered understanding and trust. It instilled in me the importance of forgiveness, both of myself and others. It nurtured empathy and compassion, guiding my interactions with others. It emphasized the interconnectedness of all humanity, fostering a sense of community and belonging. My faith wasn't just a personal belief; it was the foundation upon which I built strong and meaningful relationships.

The process of building these relationships wasn't without its challenges. Trust had to be earned, boundaries had to be established, and communication had to be cultivated. There were moments of conflict, misunderstandings, and disappointments. But the foundation of faith, mutual respect, and shared purpose allowed us to navigate these challenges and emerge stronger. We learned to communicate openly and honestly, to express our needs and vulnerabilities, and to forgive each other when necessary.

The impact of these healthy relationships on my recovery cannot be overstated. They provided a sense of purpose, a sense of belonging, and a source of strength during times of weakness. They reminded me that I wasn't alone in my struggles and that recovery was possible. They helped me to confront my past demons, to heal from old wounds, and to move forward with confidence and hope. They were an essential component of my overall well-being, contributing to my emotional, spiritual, and physical health.

Furthermore, these strong relationships have extended beyond my personal life, impacting my professional work as an addiction counselor. The empathy, compassion, and understanding I developed through my personal relationships have been instrumental in my ability to connect with clients, to build rapport, and to help them on their own journeys to recovery. The skills of active listening, emotional intelligence, and conflict resolution learned in my personal connections directly translate into the therapeutic relationship.

The network of support I cultivated extends far beyond individuals. My involvement with various recovery organizations and community groups expanded my reach and provided additional layers of connection. These organizations offer a sense of community, resources, and further opportunities for personal growth. The shared experiences within these groups allow for a sense of normalization and understanding, dispelling feelings of isolation that often accompany addiction. These communal aspects further reinforce the strength and healing capabilities found in mutual support.

The impact on my life extends even to my family relationships. Building these healthy connections helped me heal the rifts caused by my addiction. The trust and understanding fostered in my faith community and recovery circles allowed me to re-engage with my family in a more positive and constructive way. Open communication, the ability to express remorse and vulnerability, and the demonstrable commitment to recovery were key to rebuilding these vital family bonds.

In conclusion, the development of healthy and supportive relationships has been an integral part of my journey from addiction to recovery and beyond. The combination of my faith, the support of my community, and the intentional cultivation of healthy relationships has transformed my life, providing me with a sense of purpose, belonging, and lasting peace. This network of support continues to provide me with ongoing strength and encouragement, reinforcing the profound importance of these relationships. The journey is ongoing, but the relationships built along the way are a testament to the healing power of human connection and the life-giving strength of faith.

Celebrating Milestones Acknowledging Growth and Progress

The crisp autumn air bit at my cheeks as I stood on the steps of the courthouse, a small, almost imperceptible smile playing on my lips. It wasn't a grand celebration, no confetti or balloons, just the quiet satisfaction of a debt paid, a burden lifted. For years, the weight of my past mistakes had pressed down on me, a tangible manifestation of the wreckage I'd left in my wake. That day, the final payment on my restitution was made. It wasn't a magical cure-all, but it represented a tangible step towards wholeness, a concrete acknowledgment of my commitment to making amends. The feeling wasn't one of euphoria, but rather a deep, abiding peace, a quiet certainty that I was moving forward, one deliberate step at a time. My faith played a crucial role in guiding my understanding of this milestone. It wasn't about self-congratulation, but about acknowledging God's grace in allowing me to reach this point. It was a reminder that forgiveness, both from myself and others, is a process, not an event.

That same spirit of quiet gratitude accompanied another significant milestone: my first anniversary of sobriety. The temptation to dwell on the past was ever-present, a siren song whispering promises of escape. But I had learned to recognize that temptation for what it was—a test of my resolve, a challenge to my faith. Instead of succumbing to despair or self-doubt, I celebrated the victory, not with wild abandon, but with quiet reflection and prayer. I spent the day volunteering at the homeless shelter, surrounded by people whose struggles mirrored my own, offering a silent testament to the possibility of redemption. Their struggles reminded me that my own journey was far from over, but that every day was a new opportunity for growth, a chance to build upon the foundation of recovery. This anniversary wasn't merely about surviving a year without drugs; it was about thriving, about embracing life with a newfound appreciation for the small, everyday miracles.

My professional journey also offered its own set of milestones. The completion of my addiction counseling certification felt like a culmination of years of hard work, self-discipline, and unwavering faith. It wasn't just a piece of paper; it was a symbol of my transformation, a tangible representation of my commitment to helping others. The ceremony, held in a small chapel on the grounds of the university, felt almost sacred. The quiet solemnity of the occasion, the shared sense of accomplishment among my graduating class, deepened my appreciation for the journey. The act of receiving my certificate was less about personal achievement and more about a profound sense of gratitude for the opportunities I had been given. This certification wasn't an end in itself but a launching point to serve a greater purpose. I realized that my struggles had prepared me uniquely for this role, providing a level of empathy and understanding that textbooks could never teach.

These milestones, however, weren't always met with outward celebration. Some were marked by private moments of quiet reflection, times of prayer and meditation. The quiet beauty of a sunrise, the gentle rustling of leaves in a nearby park—these became my sanctuaries, spaces where I could connect with God and appreciate the progress I'd made. I found myself drawn to nature, finding solace in its enduring peace and resilience. The quiet moments were as important as the outward celebrations; they allowed me to process my emotions, to acknowledge my vulnerabilities, and to appreciate the ongoing journey of recovery. These periods of quiet contemplation often provided a deeper sense of fulfillment than the more public acknowledgments of success.

One particularly poignant milestone was the re-establishment of a relationship with my estranged brother. Years of addiction had driven a wedge between us, leaving a deep chasm of pain and resentment. His willingness to give me another chance represented an act of faith and forgiveness that touched me profoundly. Our first conversation was tentative, filled with unspoken words and lingering anxieties. But as we spoke, a sense of healing began to permeate the air, a sense of renewed hope that felt almost miraculous. The rebuilding of this relationship wasn't a sudden shift but a gradual process of trust, forgiveness, and consistent communication. The faith that had guided my recovery became a crucial bridge, connecting us across the chasm of pain and rebuilding the foundation of our relationship. It demonstrated the transformative power of forgiveness, not only for myself but for others as well.

Celebrating these milestones wasn't about self-aggrandizement; it was about acknowledging God's grace in my life. It was about recognizing that my recovery wasn't solely a product of my own will, but a testament to a higher power guiding my steps and providing unwavering support. Each achievement, however small, served as a reminder of God's faithfulness, a confirmation that He was with me through the darkest moments and had brought me to a place of hope and healing. My faith instilled in me a sense of gratitude that transcends mere personal accomplishment. It was a recognition of the profound grace and mercy extended to me, a grace I felt compelled to share with others.

This acknowledgement of God's hand in my recovery infused every milestone with a deeper meaning. The simple act of completing a daily devotional became a profound spiritual practice, a time of connection and reflection. My participation in church services wasn't just a social obligation; it was a spiritual necessity, a time to connect with a community that understood and supported my journey. Even the mundane tasks of daily living were infused with a sense of purpose, a recognition that every action, no matter how small, contributed to my overall healing and growth. The routine of daily life became a form of prayer, a silent offering of thanks and commitment.

This isn't to say the journey has been without its struggles. There are days when doubt creeps in, when the weight of the past threatens to overwhelm me. But even in those moments, my faith remains a steadfast anchor, a guiding light leading me through the darkness. The lessons learned from each setback, each stumble, have become as valuable as the moments of triumph. The setbacks become opportunities for self-reflection, for deeper understanding, and for renewed commitment. The ability to acknowledge these struggles and to approach them with humility and a renewed faith has proved vital to my continued growth.

Looking back, I see a tapestry woven with threads of joy and sorrow, triumph and failure. But the overarching theme is one of hope, a testament to the transformative power of faith and the enduring strength of the human spirit. The milestones I have celebrated are not just markers of my personal journey; they are testaments to the possibility of redemption, the potential for healing, and the enduring power of faith to guide and transform lives. The journey continues, but with each milestone, the path becomes clearer, the destination more certain, and the faith that underpins it stronger. The journey is ongoing, and the future remains unwritten, but my faith assures me that with God's grace, the path ahead will continue to be filled with hope and possibility. The future remains full of potential, and the strength to meet any challenge lies in the continued reliance on my faith. The past is not a burden to carry, but a lesson to learn from, a testament to the amazing work God has accomplished in my life.

Maintaining Sobriety Embracing LongTerm Recovery

Maintaining sobriety isn't a destination; it's a journey, a daily commitment that requires constant vigilance and unwavering faith. The first year was undeniably challenging, a constant battle against the insidious whispers of addiction, the seductive pull of the past. But as the months turned into years, I discovered a rhythm, a pattern of practices that became essential to my well-being, a spiritual and practical scaffolding that supports my continued sobriety.

One of the cornerstones of my recovery is my daily devotional. It's not just a rote recitation; it's a conversation, a time of communion with God. I find myself in the quiet stillness of early morning, before the demands of the day intrude, surrounded by the gentle light filtering through my window. I begin by acknowledging my imperfections, confessing my weaknesses, and surrendering my anxieties to God's care. Then, I immerse myself in scripture, allowing the words to seep into my soul, nourishing my spirit, and providing guidance for the day ahead. Often, a particular verse will resonate deeply, offering a message perfectly tailored to my immediate needs, a beacon of hope in moments of uncertainty. It is in these quiet moments that I find clarity and renewed resolve, a strengthening of my resolve to stay on the path of righteousness and remain sober. The devotional isn't a magic spell; it's a commitment to ongoing spiritual growth, a daily act of faith that reinforces my commitment to recovery.

My faith community plays an equally vital role in my ongoing recovery. The fellowship of believers at my church provides a supportive network, a haven where I can share my struggles and celebrate my successes without fear of judgment. The shared experience of faith creates a powerful bond, fostering empathy, understanding, and mutual support. There are times when the temptation to relapse feels overwhelming, when the weight of my past threatens to crush me. In those moments, I turn to my church community for guidance and support. Their prayers, their encouragement, their unwavering belief in my potential have been instrumental in preventing relapse. The community is more than just a social gathering; it's a spiritual family, a constant source of strength and encouragement. Attending service is not just a ritual but an act of faith, a recommitment to my spiritual journey and an affirmation of my sobriety.

Beyond the structured aspects of my faith, I find solace in the quiet beauty of nature. Spending time outdoors, surrounded by the stillness of a forest or the vastness of the ocean, allows me to connect with God on a deeper level. The natural world is a constant reminder of God's creation, of the overwhelming power and boundless love that permeates the universe. The simplicity of nature – the gentle sway of grass in the breeze, the mesmerizing rhythm of the waves – quiets the turmoil within, allowing me to find peace and serenity. These moments of quiet contemplation, often spent in prayer or meditation, help me reconnect with my spiritual center, reinforcing my commitment to sobriety and my faith in a higher power. Nature becomes a sanctuary, a space of healing and renewal, a place where I can connect with God in a profound and personal way.

Regular exercise has become another essential component of my recovery program. It's not merely about physical fitness; it's about mental and spiritual well-being. Exercise helps me manage stress, clear my head, and focus on the present moment, preventing my mind from wandering to the dark places of my past. I find that even a short walk in the park can make a significant difference in my mental and emotional state, providing a much-needed release from anxiety and stress. The physical exertion is cathartic, releasing endorphins that contribute to a sense of well-being and emotional stability. It's not merely physical; the discipline of regular exercise strengthens my resolve in other areas of my life, mirroring the perseverance required to maintain sobriety.

Maintaining a structured daily routine is vital to my recovery. This isn't about rigid adherence to a strict schedule; it's about establishing a sense of order and stability in my life. A predictable routine provides a sense of control, helping to alleviate the anxiety that can trigger relapse. This involves establishing consistent bedtimes, regular meal times, and dedicated time for prayer, meditation, and exercise. The routine helps to structure my day, providing a framework for my actions and creating a sense of predictability that counters the chaos and instability that characterized my life before recovery. This structure reduces impulsive behavior, and provides a foundation for consistent, healthy habits.

Beyond the structured elements of my recovery program, I recognize the importance of ongoing self-reflection. I regularly journal my thoughts, feelings, and experiences, allowing me to process my emotions and identify potential triggers for relapse. This practice allows me to explore my inner world, to understand my patterns of thinking, and to develop strategies for coping with stress and temptation. The act of writing is cathartic, allowing me to release my emotions and gain perspective on my challenges. The journal becomes a repository of my journey, a testament to my progress, and a source of encouragement when facing adversity. Reviewing past entries reminds me of how far I've come, reinforces my commitment to sobriety, and provides guidance in navigating future challenges.

The path to long-term recovery is not always smooth. There will be setbacks, moments of doubt, and temptations that test my resolve. But through it all, my faith remains my unwavering anchor, my guiding light. I lean on my support system—my family, my friends, my faith community—for strength and encouragement. These relationships provide crucial support during moments of crisis. The shared experiences of others struggling with addiction provide a sense of hope, reminding me that I am not alone in my journey. The shared faith builds a common foundation of support and mutual understanding, creating a sense of belonging and encouragement.

My recovery is an ongoing process, a testament to God's unwavering grace and my unwavering commitment to a better life. It's a life guided by faith, strengthened by community, and supported by a daily commitment to the principles of recovery. It's not a matter of willpower alone; it is a matter of faith, supported by a community of believers and a dedication to healthy habits. The journey continues, but with each passing day, my faith grows stronger, my resolve deepens, and my hope for the future brightens. The future holds uncertainties, but my faith in God's unwavering plan gives me the courage and strength to face whatever comes my way, knowing that I am not alone. The road to lasting recovery is paved with faith, perseverance, and the unwavering belief in the transformative power of God's grace.

The Scars That Tell a Story Embracing My Journey

The mirror reflects a stranger sometimes, a woman etched with lines that speak of hardship, of battles fought and won. These aren't just wrinkles; they're the topography of a life lived on the edge, a life scarred by addiction but redeemed by grace. Looking at my reflection, I see not defeat, but resilience. I see not shame, but triumph. The scars are a map, charting a journey from darkness to light, a testament to the transformative power of faith and the enduring strength of the human spirit.

For years, the mirror showed only a reflection of despair. My eyes were hollow, haunted by sleepless nights and the gnawing anxieties of addiction. My skin was pale and drawn, mirroring the emptiness within. Each day was a struggle, a fight for survival against the relentless grip of my demons. I carried a weight, a burden so heavy it threatened to crush me. The laughter that once filled my days was replaced by a quiet desperation, a constant fear of the next relapse, the next fall. The mirror reflected the wreckage of my life, a shattered image of who I once was, or who I thought I might have been.

The transformation wasn't instantaneous. It wasn't a sudden miracle, a flick of a switch from darkness to light. Recovery is a slow, painstaking process, a series of small victories and humbling defeats. It's a marathon, not a sprint. There were days when I felt like giving up, when the weight of my past felt unbearable, when the temptation to return to the familiar comfort of addiction was almost overwhelming. But something within me, a flicker of hope, a persistent whisper of faith, kept me going.

It was in the quiet moments of prayer, in the comforting embrace of my faith community, and in the unwavering support of my family and friends that I found the strength to persevere. It was in these spaces that I began to heal, to rebuild my life, brick by painful brick. The process was arduous, filled with self-doubt, moments of despair, and the persistent shadow of my past. But with each step forward, however small, I felt a growing sense of hope, a renewed sense of purpose.

The physical transformation was as significant as the spiritual one. The hollow eyes gained a spark, reflecting a newfound clarity and peace. The pallor faded, replaced by a healthy glow. The weight lifted, not just physically, but emotionally and spiritually. I began to rediscover the joy in simple things, the beauty of the world around me. The laughter returned, but it was a different kind of laughter, richer, deeper, born from a hard-won peace.

My scars remain, visible and invisible. The physical reminders are a testament to the battles fought, the struggles endured. But they are not marks of shame or defeat; they are badges of honor, symbols of resilience and triumph. They are reminders of how far I've come, of the transformative power of faith and the enduring strength of the human spirit. They are a story written on my skin, a narrative of redemption, a journey from darkness to light.

One of the most profound changes I experienced was the shift in my perception of myself. In the depths of my addiction, I saw myself as unworthy, unlovable, a failure. I carried a heavy burden of guilt and self-loathing. But as I embarked on my journey of recovery, I began to see myself through God's eyes, as a beloved child, worthy of love and forgiveness. This shift in perspective was pivotal in my recovery. It allowed me to embrace my flaws and imperfections, to forgive myself for the mistakes of my past, and to believe in my capacity for change and growth.

My relationship with my family underwent a profound transformation as well. The years of addiction had created a chasm between us, a deep rift of mistrust and pain. My actions had caused them immeasurable suffering, and the road to reconciliation was long and arduous. But through patience, forgiveness, and a willingness to take responsibility for my actions, we began to rebuild our relationships. The healing process was gradual, filled with moments of tenderness and understanding, but also moments of frustration and tears. The support of my family, their unwavering love and belief in me, was instrumental in my recovery. Their forgiveness was a gift that I will cherish forever.

My recovery wasn't a solo journey. It was a collaborative effort, a tapestry woven from the threads of faith, family, community, and the unwavering support of others. The shared experience of my fellow church members who had also faced struggles with addiction gave me a sense of belonging, a feeling that I wasn't alone in my journey. The collective prayers, the shared stories, the mutual encouragement created a powerful bond that sustained me through difficult times. The community provided a safe space where I could be vulnerable and honest without fear of judgment, allowing me to process my emotions and grow in faith.

The ongoing process of self-reflection remains a vital component of my recovery. My journal is not just a record of my thoughts and feelings; it's a testament to my journey, a chronicle of my triumphs and failures. It's a mirror reflecting my progress, showing me how far I've come and reminding me of the strength I possess. Reviewing my past entries provides perspective, reminding me of the challenges overcome and the lessons learned. It is a source of encouragement during difficult times, a constant reminder of my resilience and my commitment to sobriety.

The scars that tell my story are a reminder of the past, but they are also a testament to the power of redemption. They are symbols of my journey, my struggle, and my ultimate triumph. They are a narrative of hope, demonstrating the transformative power of faith, the unwavering support of a loving community, and the indomitable spirit of the human heart. My recovery is an ongoing process, a testament to the unwavering grace of God and my own persistent commitment to a life of purpose, meaning, and unwavering faith. My scars are a reminder that even from the deepest darkness, light can emerge, and that even the most shattered lives can be beautifully remade. And in those scars, I find beauty, a beauty only forged in the fires of adversity and redeemed by the grace of God. They are a map of my journey, a testament to the resilience of the human spirit, and a constant reminder of the transformative power of faith, love, and unwavering commitment to recovery. This is my story, and it's a story of hope, of redemption, and of unwavering faith in the face of adversity.

Gratitude and Hope Finding Peace and Purpose

Gratitude, a word once foreign to my vocabulary, now resides at the very core of my being. For years, my world was consumed by the insatiable cravings of addiction, a relentless pursuit of fleeting pleasure that left me empty and broken. I lived in a constant state of fear, anxiety, and self-loathing, believing myself unworthy of love, happiness, or even a second chance. The concept of gratitude was a luxury I couldn't afford, a sentiment reserved for those whose lives were untouched by the darkness that had consumed me.

But redemption, like a gentle sunrise, broke through the gloom. It wasn't a sudden, dramatic transformation, but a gradual awakening, a slow blossoming of hope in the barren landscape of my soul. It started with small things: a sunrise painting the sky with vibrant hues, the warmth of the sun on my skin, the comforting silence of a quiet morning. These were moments I had previously overlooked, too preoccupied with the relentless pursuit of my next fix to appreciate the simple beauty of existence.

The transformation began with the realization that despite the devastation addiction had wrought, there was still good in my life. My family, though wounded, still loved me, their unwavering support a lifeline in the stormy seas of my despair. My faith community, a beacon of hope in my darkest hours, offered a sanctuary of acceptance and grace, a place where I could be vulnerable and honest without fear of judgment. These were the seeds of gratitude, small but potent, taking root in the fertile soil of my recovering heart.

The daily practice of prayer became a transformative ritual, a conversation with a loving God who saw beyond my flaws, who embraced my imperfections, and who offered me unconditional love and forgiveness. It was through prayer that I learned to surrender my struggles, to let go of the guilt and shame that had held me captive for so long. It was through prayer that I discovered the profound peace that comes from trusting in a higher power, a peace that surpasses all understanding.

My gratitude extended beyond my family and faith community to the wider world. I began to see the beauty in ordinary things, to appreciate the simple joys that had once eluded me. A walk in nature became a meditation, a chance to connect with the divine in the rustling leaves, the chirping birds, and the gentle breeze. A simple act of kindness, a smile from a stranger, a helping hand offered to someone in need – these became sources of profound joy and satisfaction.

This newfound appreciation for the simple things wasn't just a feeling; it was a transformative force that reshaped my perspective, my priorities, and my life. It freed me from the self-centeredness that had characterized my addiction, opening my heart to the needs of others. I found purpose in helping others, in sharing my story, and in offering hope to those who were still struggling in the darkness.

My newfound gratitude wasn't just about appreciating the good things in my life; it was also about recognizing the lessons learned from the challenges I had faced. My addiction, though painful and destructive, had also been a catalyst for growth, a crucible in which my character was forged. It had taught me humility, resilience, and the importance of seeking help when needed. It had stripped me bare, revealing my deepest vulnerabilities, and in that vulnerability, I found strength.

The journey of recovery is not a linear path; it's filled with ups and downs, moments of triumph and moments of despair. There have been times when the old cravings have returned, when the temptation to retreat into the familiar comfort of addiction has been almost overwhelming. But with each relapse, I've learned to forgive myself, to dust myself off, and to start again. My gratitude for the grace of God, the support of my loved ones, and the resilience of my own spirit has carried me through these difficult times.

Hope, like a tenacious vine, has taken root in my heart, intertwining with my gratitude. It's a hope born not of naive optimism but of a deep-seated faith in God's plan for my life, a faith that has been tested and refined in the fires of adversity. This hope is not a passive expectation; it's an active force, driving me forward, empowering me to live a life of purpose and meaning.

The hope for the future isn't a guarantee of ease or a promise of a life without challenges. It is, rather, a steadfast belief in my ability to overcome whatever obstacles may arise. It is a recognition that even in the face of adversity, I can find strength and resilience, drawing upon the resources of my faith, my family, and my community.

My past experiences have shaped me, leaving their indelible marks upon my soul. But those scars are not symbols of shame or defeat; they are badges of honor, reminders of the battles fought and won. They are a testament to the transformative power of grace, the unwavering support of a loving community, and the resilience of the human spirit. They are a roadmap of my journey, a testament to my strength, and a constant reminder that even from the depths of despair, hope can emerge.

This hope extends beyond my own personal journey. I have a deep-seated hope for others struggling with addiction. My hope is that they, too, will find the strength and courage to seek help, to embrace their faith, and to discover the transformative power of recovery. My hope is that they will find the same peace, purpose, and gratitude that have become the cornerstones of my life.

My life, once defined by darkness and despair, is now illuminated by the radiant glow of gratitude and hope. It's a life transformed, not by some magical intervention, but by the persistent work of faith, the unwavering support of loved ones, and the unwavering commitment to a life of sobriety. My scars are a testament to the journey, a reminder of the battles fought, and a symbol of the unwavering triumph of hope over despair. It is a testament to the enduring power of the human spirit and a beacon of hope for others who may be walking a similar path. This journey, while intensely personal, offers a message of profound hope and encouragement—a testament to the restorative power of faith, the transformative nature of forgiveness, and the enduring resilience of the human spirit. The path may be arduous, filled with setbacks and challenges, but the destination, a life filled with gratitude and hope, is worth the journey. And so, I continue to walk forward, embracing the lessons learned, cherishing the blessings received, and offering my story as a testament to the unwavering power of grace and the indomitable spirit of the human heart. My journey is ongoing, but the gratitude and hope that fuel it are boundless. And in that boundless hope, I find my peace and my purpose.

A Message of Hope Inspiring Others to Find Their Path

The journey out of the abyss of addiction isn't a sprint; it's a marathon, a relentless, often grueling race against the insidious whispers of despair and the powerful pull of relapse. But I stand here today, a testament to the fact that the finish line is reachable. It's a testament to the unwavering power of faith, the transformative nature of forgiveness, and the astonishing resilience of the human spirit. My story isn't unique; countless others have traversed this difficult terrain, and countless more will follow. My hope is that my experience can offer a guiding light, a beacon of hope illuminating the path toward recovery for those still lost in the darkness.

The first, and perhaps most crucial step, is acknowledging the problem. This isn't a simple act of self-awareness; it's a profound act of surrender, a relinquishing of the control that addiction so tightly clutches. It's recognizing the powerlessness that addiction wields, the way it dictates choices, shapes behaviors, and ultimately erodes the very fabric of one's being. This admission, though painful, is the cornerstone of recovery. It allows for the acceptance of help, a vital element often overlooked in the isolating world of addiction.

Seeking help is not a sign of weakness; it's an act of incredible strength. It takes immense courage to confront the depths of one's struggles and to reach out for assistance. There is no shame in seeking professional guidance, joining support groups, or relying on the love and support of family and friends. These resources, these lifelines, are not just helpful; they are essential for navigating the complex and challenging path toward recovery.

My own recovery was deeply intertwined with my faith. Prayer became my sanctuary, my lifeline to a higher power that offered unconditional love and forgiveness. This faith, this unwavering belief in something greater than myself, provided the strength and resilience to overcome the seemingly insurmountable obstacles that addiction presented. It wasn't just about seeking divine intervention; it was about fostering a relationship with God, a nurturing connection that fostered hope, peace, and a sense of belonging.

But faith alone is not a magical cure. It's a companion on the journey, a source of strength and guidance, but it requires active participation. The journey requires diligence, discipline, and a commitment to self-improvement. This means actively engaging in therapy, attending support groups, and embracing healthy coping mechanisms. It means cultivating positive relationships, nurturing healthy habits, and surrounding oneself with a supportive community that champions one's recovery.

For me, a crucial element was the development of healthy coping mechanisms. The emptiness that addiction left behind had to be filled, but not with the fleeting highs of substance abuse. Instead, I learned to fill that void with activities that nurtured my body, mind, and spirit. Exercise became a ritual, a way to release pent-up energy and to cultivate a sense of physical well-being. Creative pursuits, like writing, allowed me to channel my emotions and experiences in a healthy and productive way. Engaging in acts of service, volunteering my time and energy to help others, became a powerful source of meaning and purpose.

The path to recovery isn't linear. There will be setbacks. There will be moments of doubt, of despair, even moments where the old cravings return with a ferocious intensity. Relapse is not a failure; it's an opportunity to learn, to adapt, and to grow stronger. It's a chance to reassess the strategies that have worked and to develop new coping mechanisms for when those old cravings strike again. Learning from mistakes is a critical part of the healing process, allowing for growth and progress.

Forgiveness is also an indispensable part of recovery. Forgiving oneself for past mistakes, for the pain and suffering caused by addiction, is crucial for breaking free from the shackles of guilt and shame. It is a powerful act of self-compassion, recognizing that everyone makes mistakes, that everyone deserves a second chance, and that healing and growth are possible. This self-forgiveness extends to others as well; releasing resentment and bitterness toward those who may have played a role in our struggles allows for a greater sense of peace and inner tranquility.

Gratitude, as I mentioned before, has become a cornerstone of my life. It's not just about appreciating the good things that have come my way; it's about recognizing the lessons learned from even the most painful experiences. My addiction, while devastating, taught me the value of humility, resilience, and the importance of seeking help. It showed me the power of forgiveness, the strength found in vulnerability, and the transformative potential of faith. This perspective shift, this capacity for gratitude, has been instrumental in my recovery, allowing me to focus on the positive aspects of my life and to appreciate the journey, even with its setbacks.

Community is vital. Surrounding myself with people who understand the struggles of addiction and who support my recovery journey has been an immeasurable gift. The fellowship of others who share similar experiences provides a sense of belonging, a feeling of not being alone in this struggle. Sharing my story with others, offering my experiences and perspective to those still struggling, has provided a sense of purpose and a way to give back to the community that helped me through my darkest hours.

My life today is a testament to the transformative power of recovery. I am not defined by my past struggles; I am defined by my resilience, by my faith, by my commitment to helping others, and by the unwavering gratitude I feel for the life I've been given. My hope is that my story will inspire others to embark on their own journey of recovery, to believe that even in the darkest moments, hope still exists, and that a life of purpose, peace, and fulfillment is within reach. The path is challenging, undoubtedly arduous, but the destination—a life free from the chains of addiction—is worth every step of the way. This is not just my message; it is my testimony, my promise, and my prayer for all those who dare to seek a brighter tomorrow.

Living a Life of Purpose Sharing My Testimony

The weight of my past, the crushing burden of addiction, once threatened to suffocate me. The darkness was absolute, a suffocating blanket woven from shame, guilt, and despair. Yet, even in that abyss, a tiny spark of hope flickered. It wasn't a sudden, dramatic epiphany, but a slow, gradual dawning of awareness – a recognition of my powerlessness and my desperate need for help. This wasn't a weakness; it was the first courageous step on a long and arduous journey.

This journey began not with a grand declaration of change, but with a whispered prayer, a desperate plea for guidance and strength from a power far greater than myself. My faith, nurtured in childhood but dormant during my years of active addiction, became my anchor in the storm. It wasn't a simple matter of believing; it was about actively cultivating a relationship with God, a daily conversation filled with repentance, gratitude, and a persistent seeking of His will. I learned to listen, not just for a dramatic divine intervention, but for the quiet whispers of guidance in the mundane moments of my life.

This newfound relationship wasn't a magic bullet, a quick fix to erase the pain and suffering of my past. Recovery required consistent, dedicated effort. It demanded active participation in my healing, a willingness to confront the root causes of my addiction, and a commitment to rebuilding my life from the ground up. This meant seeking professional help, a decision born not of weakness, but of a profound understanding of my limitations. Therapy became my safe space, a place where I could unravel the tangled threads of my past trauma and begin to heal the deep wounds that fueled my addiction.

Group therapy offered an unexpected gift: community. I found myself surrounded by people who understood my struggles, who shared similar experiences, and who offered unwavering support. The anonymity was comforting, allowing me to be vulnerable without fear of judgment. These shared stories became a source of strength, a reminder that I wasn't alone in my pain, that others had walked a similar path, and that recovery was possible. The shared laughter, tears, and moments of quiet reflection fostered a sense of belonging I had never known before. This community became my family, a chosen family bound by a shared experience and a mutual commitment to healing.

Beyond therapy and group sessions, I embarked on a personal transformation, a conscious effort to build a life rooted in purpose and meaning. The emptiness left by addiction needed filling, but not with the fleeting highs of substance abuse. This void needed to be filled with healthy habits, constructive activities, and meaningful relationships. I discovered the healing power of exercise, initially a struggle, but eventually becoming a daily ritual. The physical exertion helped to release pent-up energy and to cultivate a sense of self-discipline, a quality severely lacking during my addiction. The endorphin rush became a natural, healthy high, a replacement for the artificial highs I had previously craved.

Creative pursuits also became an integral part of my recovery. Writing, in particular, allowed me to process my emotions, to give voice to my pain and my triumphs. It became a cathartic release, a way to channel my experiences into something positive and productive. The act of writing, of transforming raw emotion into words, was profoundly healing. It was a way to reclaim my narrative, to rewrite my story from one of despair to one of hope and resilience.

Volunteering my time and energy to help others became a cornerstone of my newfound purpose. The act of serving others shifted my focus away from my own struggles, creating a profound sense of satisfaction and fulfillment. Helping others, particularly those facing similar struggles, allowed me to give back to the community that had supported me, creating a virtuous cycle of giving and receiving. This selfless service fostered gratitude, reminding me of the abundance in my life and the blessings I had been given.

However, recovery is not a linear progression. It's a winding path with unexpected twists and turns. I faced setbacks, moments of doubt, and intense cravings that tested my resolve. There were days when the whispers of despair threatened to drown out the voice of hope. Relapse became a sobering reminder that the journey is a marathon, not a sprint. But these setbacks were not failures; they were opportunities for learning and growth, chances to reassess my strategies and to develop new coping mechanisms. The lessons learned from these stumbles became powerful tools in my ongoing fight for sobriety. Each relapse served as a catalyst for introspection and a deeper commitment to my recovery.

Forgiveness, both of myself and others, was essential. Forgiving myself for the pain and suffering caused by my addiction was a crucial step in breaking free from the shackles of guilt and shame. This self-compassion allowed me to embrace my imperfections, to acknowledge my mistakes without dwelling on them, and to move forward with a renewed sense of self-worth. Forgiving others, those who may have contributed to my struggles, was equally important. Releasing the bitterness and resentment freed me from the emotional burden of the past, allowing me to experience a greater sense of peace and inner tranquility.

Gratitude became a constant companion, a way of appreciating the beauty and abundance in my life, even amidst the challenges. It was a shift in perspective, a conscious effort to focus on the positive aspects of my journey. Even the darkest experiences, the most painful memories, held valuable lessons. My addiction, though devastating, taught me the importance of humility, resilience, and faith. It showed me the power of vulnerability, the strength found in seeking help, and the transformative potential of forgiveness. This gratitude became a shield against despair, a source of strength that fueled my ongoing recovery.

Today, I stand here as a testament to the transformative power of faith, forgiveness, and community. My life is not defined by my past struggles but by the resilience I developed in overcoming them. I am grateful for the lessons learned, for the support received, and for the purpose found in helping others. My hope is that my story will inspire others to believe in their own potential for recovery, to embrace the challenges, and to find their own path to a life filled with meaning, joy, and purpose. The journey is long and arduous, but the destination – a life free from the chains of addiction – is worth every step of the way. It is a promise, a testimony, and a prayer for all who seek a brighter tomorrow. And I know, from my own experience, that brighter tomorrow awaits. The light exists, even in the deepest darkness, waiting to be discovered. This is my testimony, not just of survival, but of thriving. This is my life, transformed.

The Ongoing Journey Continuing to Grow in Faith and Recovery

The journey, I've discovered, is not a destination but a continuous unfolding, a perpetual becoming. Recovery isn't a checklist to be ticked off, a finish line to be crossed. It's a daily, sometimes hourly, commitment to choosing life, to choosing hope, even when the shadows of doubt loom large. The initial euphoria of freedom from active addiction eventually gives way to a quieter, more profound understanding: the fight for sobriety is a lifelong commitment, a constant negotiation with the self. This requires consistent vigilance, a daily recalibration of priorities, and an unwavering faith in a power greater than myself.

My faith, once a flickering candle flame in the tempest of addiction, has grown into a steady beacon, guiding my steps through the darkest nights. This deepening of my faith isn't simply about adhering to a set of religious doctrines; it's a personal relationship with God, a constant dialogue of surrender, gratitude, and a persistent seeking of His will. I've learned to find solace not just in grand pronouncements of divine intervention, but in the quiet moments of everyday grace. The beauty of a sunrise, the laughter of a child, the kindness of a stranger – these seemingly small events are filled with divine messages, reminders of God's unwavering presence in my life.

This strengthened faith extends beyond my personal relationship with God; it informs my interactions with the world. It fuels my compassion for others, particularly those struggling with addiction. Sharing my story, offering a hand to those still navigating the treacherous path, has become an integral part of my continued growth. The vulnerability of sharing my personal struggles, the raw honesty of exposing my flaws, has unexpectedly become a source of strength, both for me and for those I reach. Each shared story, each tear shed together, strengthens the bonds of community and reinforces the power of hope. The act of giving back has, in turn, been deeply rewarding, enriching my own spiritual journey in ways I could never have anticipated.

Continuing to grow spiritually means actively engaging in practices that nourish the soul. Prayer, meditation, and scripture study have become anchors in my daily routine, providing a consistent connection to the divine. These aren't just religious rituals; they are personal conversations, moments of reflection where I can process my emotions, offer my thanks, and seek guidance. They offer a sanctuary from the noise of the world, a quiet space to connect with my inner self and to cultivate a deeper understanding of God's love and grace. This inward journey has been pivotal in fostering a sense of peace and inner tranquility, a calmness that permeates every aspect of my life.

Alongside my spiritual growth, personal development has become a continuous process. This isn't about self-improvement in the superficial sense; it's about striving for wholeness, about becoming the best version of myself – a version free from the constraints of addiction and fueled by purpose and intention. This ongoing development involves regular self-reflection, a constant examination of my thoughts, feelings, and behaviors. Identifying triggers, understanding my vulnerabilities, and developing healthy coping mechanisms have become essential elements of my continued recovery. This self-awareness is crucial in preventing relapse and in navigating the inevitable challenges that life presents.

Therapy, too, remains an essential component of my ongoing journey. While I no longer attend regular group sessions, I maintain a close relationship with my therapist, utilizing her expertise whenever I face particularly challenging situations or periods of intense self-doubt. This ongoing professional guidance provides a valuable framework for navigating life's complexities and for maintaining a clear path towards continued growth. The therapeutic relationship continues to be a safe space for honest self-assessment and for exploring the nuances of my emotional landscape.

My commitment to living a life of purpose has manifested in diverse ways. Beyond writing and sharing my experiences, I've actively sought opportunities to use my skills and talents to help others. This includes volunteering at a local homeless shelter, mentoring young adults struggling with addiction, and speaking at various events to promote awareness and understanding. These activities provide a sense of fulfillment and purpose that goes far beyond personal gratification. The act of serving others strengthens my own resolve, reminding me of the abundance in my life and the privilege of using my experiences to inspire and uplift.

The power of community remains a constant source of strength. My chosen family, the individuals I met in recovery groups, continue to be a crucial part of my support system. We maintain regular contact, offering each other encouragement, accountability, and unwavering support. Knowing that I'm not alone in this journey, that there are people who understand my struggles and celebrate my successes, is profoundly reassuring. These connections offer a sense of belonging, a feeling of shared purpose that strengthens my resolve and reinforces the belief that recovery is a journey that can be navigated successfully, one step at a time.

However, I must acknowledge that the path of recovery is not without its bumps and detours. There are moments of vulnerability, times when the temptation to return to old habits is strong. These moments serve as reminders that relapse is a possibility, a reality that must be acknowledged and addressed with proactive planning and support. It's during these periods that the strength of my faith, my support system, and my commitment to personal growth become paramount. Rather than viewing these challenges as setbacks, I choose to see them as opportunities for growth, moments that reinforce the importance of consistent effort and unwavering resolve.

The ongoing journey requires consistent self-care. This encompasses a multitude of practices, including regular exercise, a healthy diet, sufficient sleep, and engagement in activities that bring joy and fulfillment. These self-care practices are not optional; they are essential for maintaining both physical and mental well-being. They help to manage stress, improve mood, and enhance overall resilience. Just as I nurture my spiritual and emotional well-being, I must also prioritize my physical health, recognizing that my overall health is essential for sustained recovery.

Forgiveness remains an ongoing process. Forgiving myself for past mistakes and forgiving others who have caused me harm are continuous acts of grace, essential for inner peace and emotional well-being. This isn't about condoning harmful behaviors; it's about releasing the burden of resentment and anger, allowing myself to move forward without being chained to the past. The process of forgiveness is a liberation, a release from the constraints of bitterness, allowing for a greater sense of freedom and tranquility.

Gratitude continues to be a constant companion, a daily practice of acknowledging the blessings in my life, both big and small. This focus on gratitude helps to shift my perspective, to recognize the abundance that surrounds me, even amidst life's challenges. It is a conscious choice to focus on the positive, to appreciate the journey, not just the destination. This daily practice fosters a sense of contentment and reinforces the belief that even in hardship, there is beauty to be found, lessons to be learned, and growth to be experienced.

Today, I stand firm in my faith, strengthened by the transformative power of recovery. My journey continues, a path of ongoing growth and discovery. It's a testament to the unwavering power of hope, the resilience of the human spirit, and the transformative potential of faith. My hope is that my story will serve as a beacon of hope for others, a testament to the possibility of transformation, and a reminder that the path to recovery, while arduous, is a journey worth undertaking. It is a life of purpose, of meaning, and of unwavering gratitude—a life transformed, and continually transforming. And that, my friends, is a promise worth living.

Acknowledgments

1. First and foremost, I offer my deepest gratitude to God, whose unwavering love and grace have been the foundation of my recovery and the inspiration for this book. Without His guiding hand, this story would not be possible. To my family, whose unwavering support and patience sustained me through the darkest book to life.

Appendix

Remember, you are not alone in this journey. Help is available.

Glossary

References

I have also a Book on Amazon, The End Was My Beginning

Author Biography

[Shawna matney] is a former addict and devout Christian who has dedicated their life to helping others find freedom from the grips of addiction. After overcoming their own struggles with [meth,cocaine, pills], they found solace and strength in faith and community support Shawna Matney is a passionate advocate for addiction recovery and recovery from trauma, sharing their story through speaking engagements, workshops, and mentoring programs. Their experience and unwavering hope have touched countless lives, inspiring others to pursue their own journeys toward healing and wholeness. Beyond their advocacy womenShawna matney enjoys Fishing,camping ,her grandchild ,family gatherings,and the lake,and finds immense fulfillment in connecting with others and sharing their message of hope and transformation.

Made in the USA
Columbia, SC
15 April 2025

56660323R00065